# LIFE AFTER THE THIRD REICH

## The Struggle to Rise from the Nazi Ruins

**PAUL ROLAND**

This edition published in 2024 by Arcturus Publishing Limited
26/27 Bickels Yard, 151–153 Bermondsey Street,
London SE1 3HA

AD006380UK

Printed in the UK

# CONTENTS

# INTRODUCTION

*Too many people here and in England hold the view
that the German people as a whole are not responsible
for what has taken place – that only a few Nazis are
responsible. That unfortunately is not based on fact.
The German people must have it driven home to them
that the whole nation has been engaged in a lawless
conspiracy against the decencies of modern civilization.*
US President Franklin D. Roosevelt

On 16 January 1945, Hitler made an unheralded return to Berlin on board his private train, the *Führersonderzug*. His reception was muted, in stark contrast to earlier official visits, when he had been greeted by a military band, deferential officials and seething crowds of adoring well-wishers.

Few risked the Allied air raids to welcome him this time.

His last gamble, the Ardennes counteroffensive, commonly known as the Battle of the Bulge, had failed, though young, inexperienced American GIs had initially been routed in the face of a German surprise attack spearheaded by heavy armour. Hitler had hoped to split the Allied advance by breaking through a thinly defended position in the American front line in the Ardennes, before pushing on to capture the strategically important port of Antwerp and in the process encircle four Allied armies. Had his strategy succeeded – and it very nearly did so – he would have been in a position to force the Western Allies to consider a ceasefire while he concentrated on repelling the Red Army in the east. But it was not to be. The Allies regrouped, dug in and repulsed repeated German assaults.

When the fog finally lifted, American planes decimated the Panzers and scattered the German infantry. Hitler had expended the reserves that could have been used to slow the Allied advance into Germany and his dream of repeating the blitzkrieg of May 1940 proved disastrous. It was now only a question of weeks before his thousand-year Reich would be consigned to history.

July 1945: British and Soviet soldiers meet up at the entrance to Adolf Hitler's bunker.

Over the following three and a half months, the Führer remained in the Chancellery and saw little of the devastation he had brought upon ordinary Berliners. In mid-March, he left his official residence for the last time and retreated underground to live in his bunker, commonly referred to as 'the concrete coffin', emerging periodically to award medals to the fanatical, underage defenders of Berlin and watch the smoke from burning buildings darken the blood-red sky. In the early hours of 29 April, he married his mistress Eva Braun in a quiet civil ceremony and on the following afternoon he said his farewells to his loyal staff. At 3.30 p.m. he retired to his study, bit down on a cyanide capsule and then shot himself in the head. Eva Braun also swallowed cyanide and died by his side.

Their bodies were carried to the shell-pitted Chancellery garden, placed in a crater, doused with petrol and set alight. There was no martial music, no elegy read at the graveside, no weeping crowds or state funeral. It was a sordid but fitting end for a man who had brought nothing but misery and untold anguish to the world.

## German surrender

A week later, on Monday 7 May 1945 at 2.41 in the morning, Hitler's successor, Grand Admiral Doenitz, ordered the unconditional surrender of the German armed forces, bringing the war in Europe to an end. The bloodiest conflict in history had lasted almost six years and claimed the lives of more than 50 million people – a number roughly equivalent to the entire population of Britain at that time. But the killing, the brutality and the suffering did not end on that day, nor in the days, weeks and months that followed.

In the immediate aftermath of the Battle of Berlin tens of thousands of German women and young girls were raped and brutalized by soldiers of the Red Army. Thousands more committed suicide rather than suffer the same fate, while others subsequently killed themselves because they could not live with the shame of having been violated.

British officers entering the wealthy suburbs of West Berlin on 4 July were appalled to find hundreds of bloated female bodies floating in the lakes. But somehow the survivors found the will to live, despite it all.

Few Germans escaped unscathed or remained unchanged by their wartime experiences. Civilians and combatants alike were affected to some degree by what they had seen or suffered. For some, their physical wounds would heal, but the psychological scars would take longer. Many never recovered.

## Camp horrors revealed

Even before the horror of the concentration camps became public knowledge and the general population were damned for their complicity in the crimes committed by the regime, many ordinary Germans felt only disgust for their leaders. Housewife Hildegard Wortmann reacted to the news of Hitler's suicide on 30 April by calling him 'a lousy, bloody coward'. And she was not alone in thinking that he had taken the easy way out.

One anonymous Berliner spoke for many when she expressed her feelings of bitterness and betrayal towards the Nazis.

*The first time I had hatred for Hitler was not hatred against the terror regime, but hatred like against gangsters. Hitler promised us to win half of the world and he asked us to help him and so we have done and now we have nothing.*

Those Germans who had been political opponents of the regime and so were accused of being enemies of the state – the so-called 'undesirables' and 'outsiders' – were liberated from the concentration camps, the slave labour camps and the Gestapo prisons.

It wasn't only the Jews who had suffered. As many as 250,000 Romany people had been murdered in the camps, as well as three million Poles among a huge number of others. Countless victims whose names would never be known had been tortured, starved, beaten and exterminated for their religious beliefs, their political opposition to the regime and even for their sexual orientation. Some had been condemned on the mere word of a spiteful neighbour or other informant.

In total, more than 14 million people had died as a direct result of Hitler's *Vernichtungskampf* (war of annihilation) against the Slavs and his *Rassenkampf* (war of racial extermination) against the Jews.

In Auschwitz the four main gas chambers could each hold up to 2,000 people. The marshland behind the camp where their ashes and remains were hastily deposited is today ten feet thick in human bonemeal.

Only 700,000 survived the camps, but their ordeal was not over. They then had to choose between trying to rebuild their lives in the midst of their former persecutors or turning their back on their country to start a new life elsewhere.

## Starving civilians

Hitler had boasted that the Third Reich would last a thousand years, but it had been brought to a devastating and ignominious end just 12 years later. And yet some former members of the Hitler Youth were not prepared to admit defeat. They belonged to the underground of fanatical resistance fighters known as the Werewolves, who were willing to continue 'the struggle' long after the official surrender. They would use their youth to lure unsuspecting GIs into lethal traps.

According to US Army instructional films and booklets, pretty Fräuleins posed a far more serious threat to young soldiers than the risk of contracting a social disease.

*You'll see a lot of good-looking babes on the make there. German women have been trained to seduce you. Is it worth a knife in the back?*

But it was hard to turn your back on starving, frightened faces, especially for the younger replacements who had been sent to Germany after D-Day and hadn't fought their way through France or been besieged at the Battle of the Bulge in the winter of 1944. What harm could there be in giving the kids chocolate and sweets and the young women cigarettes, some spare rations or even silk stockings? So soldiers from the occupying armies continued to be killed or maimed on German soil in the weeks and months after 7 May 1945.

It is believed that approximately eight million Germans perished during the war, of whom over five and a half million were combatants and around two million were civilians. The

Russians took three million German POWs into captivity, of whom only a third returned alive, and a further three million Germans would die after VE Day.

Germany's towns and cities had been all but obliterated and the population was reduced to starvation level. Its infrastructure was also wrecked. It is said that on the night of 25–26 April Hitler had ordered the flooding of the U-Bahn (underground railway) tunnels to drown the advancing Russians, knowing that thousands of Berliners were sheltering there and that wounded German soldiers in hospital trains parked in the tunnels would also be among the victims. As many as 15,000 Germans are believed to have died as a direct result of his last vindictive act. And 12,000 perished from malnutrition in Berlin alone during that first year of peace. The first summer after the war the anti-Nazi theologian Otto Dibelius told his congregation that the mortality rate in Berlin was then four times higher than it had been during the Allied air raids.

And yet news of the Germans' privations failed to elicit much sympathy in Britain, where the population had sacrificed so much already and were still enduring the misery of rationing. Despite the apparent unwillingness of the average British person to be charitable to their former enemy, some 96,000 tons of food were sent by Britain to Germany every month, while Russia sent twice that amount to Berlin in the first 12 weeks of peace.

But it was woefully inadequate. By July 1946 the British-controlled Central Office for Nutrition and Agriculture in Germany was forced to reduce the ration for civilians from a barely sufficient 1,200 calories a day to almost half that amount.

Many were driven to eat horse meat (some of it decomposing) when they were fortunate enough to find it, but so many animals were infected with disease that butchering them was a risky business. Food was so scarce that the population had resorted to growing vegetables in their window boxes and anywhere else that was out of the reach of their starving neighbours.

## Social chaos

*[Millions] were living in medieval fashion surrounded by the broken down machines of the 20th century.*
Anne O'Hare McCormick, *New York Times*

It was the lack of food as much as anything which finally convinced the Western Allies that they had to help Germany get back on its feet if they wanted to avoid having to expend their own limited resources policing and subsidizing the country. As the British historian and author Frederick Taylor observed in *Exorcising Hitler*:

*It [...] came from a dawning realization that unless Germany was allowed to work, and produce, to an extent resembling her pre-war capacity, the country would forever be a [...] mendicant nation dependent on the victors for its physical survival. A nation that might then, as it had after 1918, turn viciously against its tormentors.*

Of more immediate concern was the distinct possibility that the Russians might increase their influence in Europe by making life in East Germany more attractive to the migrating masses, a fear articulated by America's viceroy in Germany, General Clay.

*It is my sincere belief that our proposed ration allowances in Germany will not only defeat our objectives in middle Europe, but will pave the road to a communist Germany.*

As abhorrent as the idea might have been to the displaced and dispossessed, the Soviet-controlled sectors were offering substantially higher rations than were to be had in the British, American and French zones. For a starving people it was

Post-war Berlin and boys are served up with a portion of gruel (flour and milk) in their school in the central district of Charlottenburg. Rations were provided by the British authorities.

tempting to take their chances with the Russians – at least you might live another day.

The most fertile farming land was now in the East and the Russians were efficient in distributing supplies, despite the disruption to the road and rail network. As Victor Sebestyen notes in *1946 – The Making of the Modern World*:

*... when food stocks were low, the Soviets sent extra supplies to Germany, even during the winter of 1945–46, when famine ravaged much of the USSR and more than a million and a half Soviet citizens starved to death. In the Soviet-controlled sector of Germany, hunger abounded, but there was almost no starvation.*

In the cities under Allied control the triple scourge of dysentery, diphtheria and typhoid posed a serious threat to public health. Children were running wild in the rubble and crime was rampant, with looting routinely blamed on some of the seven million 'displaced persons' who were on the move in search of surviving relatives, or what was left of their former homes. In addition, there were gangs of former Russian POWs and six million former slave labour workers roaming the country, which contributed to a wave of terror, intimidation and theft. Two hundred and forty incidents of robbery a day were reported in Berlin and the true figure must have been significantly higher.

## Child victims of war

Sadly, it was the children who were driven to risk serious injury to steal the essentials for survival: food and coal. Hospitals reported a dramatic increase in the number of children seeking treatment for lacerations to their hands and in some cases even severed fingers, suffered while they had been attempting to steal from passing army trucks. The soldiers guarding the load had lashed out with bayonets, with the inevitable result.

Civil law and order had effectively broken down and it was practically impossible to identify or trace the perpetrators of random attacks as identification papers had been lost or forged and those which were produced as proof could not be relied upon.

Crossing into another zone required an Interzone Pass and this prevented many perpetrators from seeking anonymity in a different military zone. Besides, it was easier to melt into the mass of migrants than get through the manned border crossings. But the greatest obstacle to maintaining order was the sheer number of people on the move.

Four and a half million refugees from the East would soon flood into the already over-populated British zone, which extended from Düsseldorf in the south to Kiel in the north, and in such a seething mass of humanity it was easy to lose oneself.

Many of the buildings that were still standing were unsafe or uninhabitable, posing further hardship for those seeking shelter from the onset of the first post-war winter, which was fortunately uncharacteristically mild. In Germany alone 3.6 million homes had been destroyed, leaving 7.6 million people homeless. Ninety-three per cent of homes in Düsseldorf were uninhabitable, compared with 66 per cent in Cologne, 53 per cent in Hamburg, 51 per cent in Hanover and 60 per cent in Dortmund.

Many Allied observers were shocked at the scale of destruction they saw in the German cities, which often far exceeded the damage visited upon London, Coventry or Bristol during the Blitz. More high explosives were dropped on Duisburg, for example, in two days in October 1944 than had been dropped on London during the 11 months between September 1940 and July 1941 and 40,000 tons of shells were fired by Soviet artillery in the final battle for Berlin. This was the inevitable consequence of the 'Total War' Goebbels had called for on 18 February 1943.

The Allies aroused some resentment by requisitioning the best accommodation for themselves and in Berlin 3,000 houses and apartments were taken over and the occupants evicted. The few schools that managed to open were woefully understaffed, with one teacher for every 70 pupils (the result of so many teachers having been prohibited from returning to their posts on account of their membership of the Nazi Party). Within a year 90 per cent of them had to be reinstated but teaching was still difficult when there were hardly any textbooks to go around. Added to that, far too many pupils fell asleep from hunger during lessons and in bad weather they didn't bother to go to school at all because there was no coal for the heating systems and few of the children had shoes.

The plight of the children was particularly painful to see. They scavenged in packs and were so filthy that it was said that the only clean part of them was the whites of their eyes.

Both their physical and emotional growth was stunted and they were showing symptoms of poor diet, lack of sleep and the first signs of psychological disorders which would manifest in the months and years to come. They were also suffering from what had been known as shell shock or what would later be classified as post-traumatic stress disorder. Bad teeth could be fixed and sores, tuberculosis and rickets were treatable, but emotional disorders such as depression, chronic anxiety and nervous ailments would require years of therapy and they did not belong to a generation that would have considered seeking help.

## Nation of beggars

The soft-hearted British and American soldiers felt bound to share their rations with these war orphans, even though the German soldiers had not shown any pity for the children in the ghettos and villages of Eastern Europe. There were 15 million children needing to be fed, clothed and educated. Two and a half million of these grew up without fathers and 250,000 were orphans. Half of the children in Berlin were showing the symptoms of rickets and among the adults there were 1,000 new cases of typhoid recorded every month, 2,000 cases of diphtheria and an epidemic of various illnesses resulting from malnutrition.

American CARE (Cooperative for American Remittances to Europe) packages provided food, warm blankets and clothing for some, but it was mainly down to the efforts of individual humanitarians to beg, borrow and requisition whatever they could to re-educate a generation of German children whose welfare was not an Allied priority.

The Reichsmark was worthless, so the economy was reduced to bartering and the black market. Germans, who had once prided themselves on belonging to an orderly nation, now scrambled

scrambled for standing room in the trams and crowded on to the U-Bahn and sallow men shadowed the 'Amis' (nickname for the Americans) in the hope of snatching up a discarded cigarette butt. The Master Race had been reduced to a nation of beggars.

All semblance of normal life had been erased. Midnight on 8 May 1945 was Germany's Year Zero or, as the Germans themselves called it, '*Stunde Null*' ('Zero Hour'). As one German woman remarked, 'When the war is over, it is only the shelling, the shooting and the bombing that stops. The war to survive continues and the struggle to recover begins. Life does not return to normal just because the fighting has stopped.'

*A great war leaves a country with three armies: an army of cripples, an army of mourners, and an army of thieves.*
Anonymous German

## Chapter One

# COLLAPSE

## April 1945

As Hitler's thousand-year Reich crumbled, three million British and American troops and their allies converged on the heartland of National Socialism from the west and more than six and a half million Soviet troops descended on Berlin, the capital of Hitler's empire, from the east. The Red Army were, in the main, merciless and unforgiving after losing more than 11 million men and having witnessed the brutality meted out to their people by the Germans. The SS had been particularly, but not exclusively, involved in this. A quarter of the population of Belorussia (modern-day Belarus) had perished in what Communist Russia would commemorate as 'The Great Patriotic War'.

Now they were at the mouth of what the Soviet press called 'the lair of the fascist beast' and were encouraged to vent their anger on the population. Posters incited them with slogans: 'Soldier, have you killed your German today?' and 'You are now on German soil. The hour of revenge has struck.' *Krasnaya Zvezda*, the official Soviet military newspaper, declared:

*The Germans are not human beings. From now on the word 'German' is for us the worst imaginable curse … If you have not killed at least one German a day, you have wasted that day.*

The Russians had been the first to liberate the death camps of Eastern Europe where Slavs, Soviet prisoners and Hitler's political opponents had starved and endured inhuman treatment, but as early as July 1944 Hitler's death factories were common knowledge, following the discovery of Majdanek concentration camp outside Lublin.

In their haste to save their skins, the SS guards had ignored Himmler's orders to demolish the gas chambers and the

Two Russian soldiers manhandle a girl in the SBZ, which was the German zone under Soviet command, in 1945 or 1946.

crematoria and scatter the mounds of ash and human bone fragments that testified to the extermination of countless victims. The scale of the enterprise had prevented the timely disposal of damning evidence – the guards had left behind hundreds of thousands of pairs of spectacles, shoes, suits, coats, dresses, suitcases and toys, all of which had belonged to those who had ended their journey at this accursed place. Majdanek was an immense warehouse where the personal items abandoned by those who passed through Sobibór, Treblinka and Belzec were taken to be sorted and transported back to Germany to clothe evacuees. Equally incriminating were the detailed records that had not been destroyed when the SS members abandoned the camp.

## Mixed response to camp reports

The Soviet propaganda machine made the most of these discoveries, providing an added incentive – if one were needed – for the Red Army to wreak their revenge on the Germans, military and civilians alike.

In November 1944, a full six months before the Red Army besieged Berlin, the magazine *Znamya* (Banner) published a highly emotive but chillingly accurate description of the killing process at Treblinka. Although the average Russian soldier probably didn't care about the fate of the Jews, he would have recognized the names of the towns and cities where the victims had been rounded up and transported to the killing factory. And he would have known that among them were comrades from Warsaw, Bialystok, Siedlce, Lomza and Belorussia.

*Himmler's minions are now telling the story of their*
*crimes – a story so unreal that it seems like the product*
*of insanity and delirium … It was not without reason*
*that Himmler began to panic in February 1943; it was*
*not without reason that he flew to Treblinka and gave*
*orders for the construction of the grill pits followed*
*by the obliteration of all traces of the camp. It was not*
*without reason – but it was to no avail. The defenders*
*of Stalingrad have now reached Treblinka; from the*
*Volga to the Vistula turned out to be no distance at*
*all. And now the very earth of Treblinka refuses to be*
*an accomplice to the crimes the monsters committed.*
*It is casting up the bones and belongings of those*
*who were murdered; it is casting up everything*
*that Hitler's people tried to bury within it …*

Not all of Stalin's soldiers were peasants and brutes. There
were artists, intellectuals, academics and professionals too and
800,000 women served in the Red Army, a quarter of whom
were decorated for bravery. Two thousand of these served as
snipers and such accounts of cruelty against Slavic women and
children must have stirred their thirst for revenge.

By contrast, the British and American press and broadcasters
were highly sceptical of such reports. Even when one of their
own reporters submitted an eyewitness account of Majdanek,
the BBC refused to broadcast it, believing that it was another
example of Soviet propaganda. The *New York Herald Tribune*
rejected the same report with the comment that it sounded
'inconceivable'.

## The vengeance to come

The Russian press knew what the Nazis were capable of, having uncovered the massacre of nearly 34,000 civilians at Babi Yar in Kiev in September 1941 and having seen the aftermath of numerous other atrocities as the Russian Army pushed the Germans back to the outskirts of Berlin. A month later, on 17 December 1944, *Pravda* accused all Germans of complicity in the crimes of the Third Reich.

*For many years the Nazis brainwashed German youth. What were they conveying to the little fascists? A feeling of superiority. Now the world knows what racial or national arrogance means. If every nation decided that they are first in the world and therefore have the right to order others about, we will see new Majdaneks in the 20th century.*

*In the countries they captured, the Germans killed all the Jews: the elderly and nursing babies. Ask a captured German why did your compatriots annihilate six million innocent people? And he will say: 'They are Jews. They are black (or red) haired. They have different blood.' This began with vulgar jokes, with name-calling by hoodlums, with graffiti, and all this led to Majdanek, Babi Yar, Treblinka, to ditches filled with children's corpses ... People all over the world need to remember that nationalism is the road to Majdanek ... fascism was born out of the greed and stupidity of some, and the perfidy and cowardice of others. If mankind wants to put an end to the bloody nightmare of these years, it must put an end to fascism ... Fascism – a terrifying cancerous tumour ... When* Die Pommersche Zeitung *dares to claim that the Germans crossed their borders as the most peaceful missionaries, it means that the fascists now have only one hope: the loss of memory ... We must remember: this is our obligation to the dead heroes and to the children.*

Expressing hatred for all Germans and vowing to avenge the sufferings of his people, one Russian soldier remarked: 'Hitler robbed the whole of Europe ... the Germans deserve the atrocities they unleashed.' The Germans themselves sensed and dreaded what was to come. A common phrase was repeated all over the eastern regions as the Russians closed in: 'If they do to us what we have done to them, God help us!'

## German prosperity

Once across the German border, the Russian troops were infuriated to find the shops stocked with goods stolen from stores, farms and factories in the occupied territories. Lieutenant Boris Itenberg wrote to his wife: 'How well these parasites lived. I saw ruined houses, abandoned furniture, dozens of other signs of an incredibly good life. They lived so well. Why did they need more?'

His resentment was echoed by infantry officer Dimitry Shchegolev: 'The more we penetrate into Germany, the more we are disgusted by the plenty we find everywhere.'

In the West, the Americans witnessed similar scenes of prosperity, at least in the agricultural regions where even the farm animals were well fed. They passed by 'rich', well-equipped and well-managed farms tended by 'strong and healthy' farmers and their equally well-fed and well-nourished foreign workers. It was only when the Americans entered the larger towns and cities that they witnessed the destruction and sensed the 'air of defeat'.

When they came upon ragged groups of slave workers wandering aimlessly in the countryside, they directed them to a US storehouse where they were issued with clothing and food. Eighteen-year-old Pole Bogdan Moszkowski recalled watching the reaction of his fellow refugees and former slave workers to seeing such plenty after so many years of privation. It was theirs for the asking.

*In the stores many clothes remain. No one takes more than one set, but every one of them takes as much food as he can carry. They want to be surrounded with food – they do not want to part with it – they want to see it all the time.*

## City under siege

The fighting in both sectors was fierce now that the war was being fought on German soil and the Russians knew that they would probably bear the brunt of it when they reached the capital. Berlin was a citadel covering 300 square miles and it was fortified by defences 30 miles deep, so it would not fall without a prolonged and costly fight. All German citizens, male and female, young and old, were compelled to enlist in the *Volkssturm* (People's Militia), if they were not already in uniform, and were then ordered to fight to the death for Führer and Fatherland. A further 100,000 Soviet soldiers would die taking the city and 350,000 would be grievously wounded.

The city's three million inhabitants had been under siege for more than a year, first by incessant Allied air raids and now by massed artillery. They were demoralized by the unceasing bombardment, the disruption of gas and electricity and the scarcity of food, fresh water and essential supplies, added to which they lived like cornered rats in bombed-out buildings where insanitary conditions and the presence of decomposing bodies made life intolerable. On top of all of that, they existed in a constant state of fear, not only because of the shelling but also due to the Nazi fanatics who roamed the streets executing deserters and those who refused to fight.

In the face of imminent defeat and retribution, Berliners exhibited their characteristic gallows humour. They referred to their LSR air raid shelters (*Luftschutzraum*) as an abbreviation for *Lernt schnell Russisch* (Learn Russian Quickly), while graffiti appeared on shrapnel-pitted walls urging Berlin's citizens to 'Enjoy the war, peace will be terrible'.

## Division of Berlin

The fate of Berlin had been decided at the Yalta Conference in February 1945, when Churchill, Roosevelt and Stalin had called for Germany's unconditional surrender, the demilitarization of its armed forces and the division of the capital. The Big Three had also redrawn the map of post-war Europe, which saw Poland coming under Soviet rule, despite the fact that the

Western Allies had initially gone to war to ensure its sovereignty. But Stalin reminded them that Poland had provided an invasion route to Russia on three previous occasions and he could not risk this happening again.

The plan to divide a defeated Germany into four military zones was only intended to be a temporary measure, to enable the orderly administration of the country and its capital. Although the Soviets could have refused to share Berlin with their allies, as they did with Poland, they needed their cooperation to secure 20 billion dollars in reparations. However, such a sum was more than a rejuvenated Germany could ever hope to pay.

The Soviets were against borrowing from a capitalist democracy on principle and the American corporations would have demanded the right to set up subsidiaries in the USSR, so the Russians had to resort to stripping Germany and Eastern Europe of its plant and machinery and other assets to recover their losses. Stalin's only concession was to agree to hold elections in the Soviet zone of post-war Germany, but only on the understanding that the result would be to endorse the Communist administration.

## Berlin left to the Soviets

The big question was what to do with a defeated Germany and how to ensure that it did not become belligerent in the future. As Berlin was the symbolic heart of the Nazi state and a key objective, its capture became a priority. Whoever occupied the greater part of Berlin when Germany surrendered would control the city and be in the strongest position when it came to negotiating the partition of the country.

Unfortunately, while Stalin could dictate military strategy and order his generals to direct all their forces to the capital, the Allied commanders had to contend with politicians who had conflicting requirements and priorities.

General Dwight D. Eisenhower was within 200 miles (320 km) of Berlin in the spring of 1945 when both US General Patton and British General Montgomery urged him to authorize their forces to take the capital, but Eisenhower declined, believing it to be 'not worth the trouble'. Instead, he ordered the British and American troops under his command to encircle the Ruhr valley to seize the core of German industry.

In doing so they would trap 400,000 German troops, a decisive victory in military terms, but one which would not strengthen the hand of their political masters when they sat around the negotiating table. Eisenhower came in for considerable criticism for refusing to move on Berlin when he had the chance, but he argued that taking the city would have resulted in considerable losses at a time when the war was practically won and, besides, President Roosevelt had promised Stalin that the Soviets could have first crack at the city. Eisenhower was therefore wary of being embroiled in a political storm.

## Calm before the storm

The threat of a Russian-dominated Europe was not much of a concern at the time to the Americans, who believed that the Atlantic made invasion impossible. Churchill, however, was extremely distrustful of Stalin, with whom he had violently disagreed over the fate of the German POWs. Stalin had wanted to execute 50,000 of them in cold blood in retaliation for the

Dwight Eisenhower is shown the tunnel leading to the Citadel of Jülich in the Rhineland. Churchill and Montgomery were also in town in March 1945, posing for propaganda photos after the Allies' hard-won triumph here.

suffering inflicted on his people, although he later claimed to have intended that as a joke.

Another factor that may have played a part in Eisenhower's decision not to go for Berlin was the knowledge that American troops would have to be redeployed in the Pacific as soon as victory over Nazi Germany was assured, so America would need all the battle-hardened men it could muster to fight the Japanese. General Omar Bradley defended Eisenhower's decision by saying that it would have been too stiff a price to pay for a prestige objective, one that they would eventually have to concede to the Soviets under the terms of the Yalta accord.

By the time Berlin had fallen on 2 May, the Russians had lost an additional 80,000 soldiers (some sources estimate 100,000), a figure which the British and Americans would have felt was too great a sacrifice. The next day, loudspeaker vans drove through the ruins announcing that the city was now in Soviet hands and that all resistance must cease. As one Berliner recalled, there was an unnatural silence during which the beleaguered population emerged cautiously from their cellars and the rubble, grateful that their ordeal was finally over but knowing that another was just about to begin.

## The rape of Berlin

*Understand it if a soldier who has crossed thousands of kilometres though blood and fire and death has fun with a woman or takes some trifle ... We lecture our soldiers too much; let them have their initiative.*
Joseph Stalin

The women of Berlin were considered part of the spoils of war by the Russians. None were safe, not even young girls and grandmothers. The Soviet soldiers saw it as their right to do as they wished, to satiate their lust and to loot and drink themselves into a stupor. They did it partly out of revenge and partly, perhaps, to shock themselves out of the numbness that followed four years of killing and being killed.

For several days they were let off the leash and could not be controlled, even by their own officers. Although they may have been factory workers or farm labourers back in Mother Russia, in Berlin they were the masters. They had all been brutalized by their experiences and some were consumed by a desire to abuse those they blamed for everything they had seen and suffered. Many, however, were merely brutes who thought nothing of exploiting the opportunity to force themselves on their defenceless prey.

It was rumoured that Stalin had issued an order granting his men permission to rape German women in order to break their spirit and populate post-war Germany with tens of thousands of future comrades, the so-called *Russenbabies*. As many as 200,000 of these children were born, it is believed, despite the large number of crude abortions carried out, many by the women themselves without the aid of an anaesthetic. Abortion was illegal in Germany under Article 218 of the penal code, but an exception was made for the women who became pregnant as a result of the mass rapes in 1945.

In a desperate attempt to avoid the inevitable, many German women made themselves as unattractive as possible. They smeared dirt and ashes on their faces, painted sores and other physical symptoms of disease on their bodies and did anything else they could to appear old and unappealing, but the Russians were not fussy. With a terrible irony, some of the women sewed the yellow star of David on to their clothes in an attempt to pass themselves off as '*Juden*' (Jews), but the Russians did not discriminate and raped them anyway.

As one Russian soldier admitted in a letter home, dated February 1945: 'They do not speak a word of Russian, but that makes it easier. You don't have to persuade them. You just point a revolver and tell them to lie down.'

The women of Berlin and other towns occupied by the Red Army soon came to fear the only two German words their tormentors knew: '*Frau, komm!*' ('Come, woman!') Children soon adopted the phrase in a macabre new game, with the boys playing the role of the Russians and their female playmates acting the part of the victims.

Curiously, the presence of children prevented some of the Russians from carrying out their intentions. As several historians have noted, the mere presence of children was sometimes sufficient to dissuade the more sentimental Russians from carrying out barbaric attacks.

They were also susceptible to petitioning from weeping children who had been sent by their parents to make a plea for special treatment, or for the family to be exempt from eviction. Ten-year-old Helga Feyler was sent to scrounge food from the Russians near her village with her baby brother in her arms, as her grandmother had assumed that the 'Ivans' wouldn't give anything to an adult but they might find something for two adorable children. Helga was fortunate to meet a Russian soldier who showed her a photograph of his son and told her in broken German that he was a father and wanted to hold her brother. He swung the infant around and fondled his hair then handed him back as soon as the baby started to cry. Helga returned with two loaves of bread, sugar and a little meat.

Children grew up quickly in such circumstances; many ran wild beyond parental control as their parents, who had followed the false doctrines of Hitler, lost confidence in their own beliefs and, with that, authority over their offspring.

*Lost honour*

Many women were raped multiple times and by more than one man. Whole platoons took turns and the injuries inflicted were as horrific as the ordeal itself, especially when the rapist was too drunk to satisfy himself and used the bottle he'd been drinking from instead. But the soldiers of the Red Army did not see themselves as beasts and when several of their victims who had been gang-raped in Königsberg begged their attackers to shoot them, the Russians responded by saying that only German soldiers shoot women.

The orgy continued into May. On the last day of that month anti-Nazi resistance member Ruth Andreas-Friedrich wrote in her diary:

*Inge Zaun lives in Klein-Machnow. She is 18 years old and didn't know anything about love. Now she knows everything. Over and over again, 60 times ... Suicide is in the air. 'Honour lost, all lost', a bewildered father says, and hands a rope to his daughter, who*

*has been raped 12 times. Obediently, she goes and
hangs herself from the nearest window frame.*

Many German men were forced to stand by and watch while
their women were repeatedly raped, though some of the boys
successfully defended their sisters and their mothers. Some of
the victims were sufficiently strong to survive the ordeal and
put it behind them but others were destroyed by it. Many
more were traumatized, but in time they came to think of it as
something unspeakable that had happened to someone else, the
person they had once been.

A number of victims simply resigned themselves to their fate
and hoped that their passivity or apparent willingness would
reduce the ferocity of the attack. In the overcrowded cellars
where women huddled together in fear of the next assault, word
soon spread that one sure way to minimize the distress was to
attach themselves to a high-ranking Russian officer and hope
that he would protect them.

Berliner Friedrich Luft had the presence of mind to pretend
that two dead women in the next apartment were his wife and
daughter, which elicited sympathy from the Russians, who
prayed over them and brought the bereaved father small gifts
of food and drink.

## Savage acts of aggression

It wasn't only in Berlin. The horror was repeated in Silesia,
Pomerania and East Prussia, where tens of thousands of women
were raped and murdered. In *A Terrible Revenge*, Cuban-

American diplomat and academic Alfred de Zayas cites one particularly distressing example which must stand for countless similar incidents.

In the village of Baerwalde, a group of Russian soldiers took turns raping Marie Naumann in a hayloft while their comrades garrotted her children. Her husband was forced at gunpoint to watch, then he and his wife were hanged. Marie was rescued and revived by Polish civilians, but they attacked her when she told them that the Russians had done it and not the Germans as they had thought. She then fled to a friend's home, where she was raped by a Russian officer and shortly afterwards by another group of Russians, who beat her so badly that the next bunch of soldiers to find her turned away in disgust.

In all, there were an estimated two million rapes in Germany, up to 100,000 in Vienna and tens of thousands in Hungary, pro-Nazi Romania and Bulgaria, all of them savage acts of aggression, violence and revenge.

In addition to the trauma of rape and the fear of pregnancy, there was the scourge of sexually transmitted diseases and a shortage of antibiotics with which to treat them. But the issuing of food rationing stamps was conditional on the women obtaining a medical certificate confirming that they had received treatment for STDs.

The incidents of rape and looting eventually diminished as the Soviet commanders reined in their men and regained control, aware of the damage it was doing to the Russians' prospects of winning the first free elections which were to be held that summer.

## Not just the Russians

The Russians were not the only soldiers to let victory go to their heads. On 17 April units of the French 2nd Army Corps took the town of Freudenstadt in the Black Forest. After shelling the undefended town, they set fire to over 600 homes, shops and public buildings before indulging in a three-day orgy of looting, rape and wanton destruction. Seventy inhabitants were killed and 600 women later sought treatment for rape and violent assault in the town's hospital, which itself had been the scene of an armed attack. Patients had had their valuables taken and one patient, a Frenchman, was shot dead in his bed.

Stuttgart, Vaihingen and Tübingen were among other German towns whose citizens later claimed to have suffered under their French liberators. At the time the blame was attributed mainly to the Moroccans, as the French authorities attempted to distance themselves from the actions of their soldiers and possibly scapegoat certain parties, but there were Algerians and members of the Foreign Legion and the French 5th Armoured Division among the troops who had run riot in Freudenstadt.

None of the Allies could claim to be entirely blameless in this regard. American GIs had also exploited the situation, while the British were characteristically more reserved and generally regarded as behaving like 'gentlemen', although they too had their share of 'bad apples' who had abused their power. Court-martial records reveal that several hundred American and French soldiers were accused of raping German women.

There were over 400 rape charges against US personnel recorded in March 1945, 500 more in April, half that number in the following month and then less than 50 in each of the succeeding months, as consensual relationships became the norm. The Americans were harsher than their allies in sentencing convicted rapists, with a number of soldiers being executed for their crimes.

Although 94,000 *Besatzungskinder* ('children of the occupation') were born in the American zone, it was only half as many as had been conceived as a result of rape by the Russians. However, as soon as the ban on marriage between US personnel and German women was relaxed in December 1946, the exodus of GI brides to the United States began, with 14,000 of them in the first rush.

As abhorrent as the actions of the occupation armies had been in regard to rape, looting and random acts of violence, it would be unrealistic to expect military discipline to be maintained under such circumstances. Nevertheless, the fact that the rapes went on for so long and appear to have been condoned by the Red Army commanders is both shameful and inexcusable.

## Fascination with GIs

The American soldiers held a strange fascination for many young German women who had been denied the pleasure of watching Hollywood movies, reading American magazines and listening to American music (especially big band swing) for 12 dispiriting years.

Black GIs were not discriminated against like they were back home where a 'color bar' operated. When it came to intimacy with their new 'Amis' from the US, German women could escape austerity and enjoy a few of life's luxuries imported from the States, but some of them became pregnant. The problem came with the girls' parents, who would refuse to bring up a mixed-race baby, and so the 2–3,000 such infants born to German women in the late 1940s were frequently given up for adoption.

Some German girls were even prepared to forgo their ingrained prejudice against Jewish GIs if they needed the coffee, chocolate and other items badly enough, although the men were not so easily bought. Felix Putterman, a Jewish artilleryman, had been through hell the day he was propositioned and brusquely refused the offer of sex, informing the woman that she wouldn't want him as he was a Jew, whereupon she replied: 'Oh, but you are a white Jew.'

The stereotype worked the other way around too. Lieutenant Colonel Byford-Jones, a British officer on Montgomery's staff in Berlin, had been shocked by the typical American soldier's view of German women. One told him:

*Somehow or other we'd been led to believe that a German girl was fat and ugly, with fanged teeth, who beat her fist on* Mein Kampf *and shouted 'Heil Hitler, I am a Nazi'. (Psychological warfare and scientific orientation had told him everything about the Germans, except that they were human beings.)*

## Aftermath

*The city was deserted, the grey of the sky seemed to run in the streets and, from the height of a man, you could look out over all the roofs; in order to find the streets*

*under the ruins, they had cleared away and piled up the debris; in the cracks of the asphalt, grass had started to grow. Silence reigned, and each noise, in counterpoint to it, underlined it even more; the bittersweet odour of rotting organic material constituted a solid wall through which one had to pass; you floated over Berlin.*
Roberto Rossellini, 1955 (*Cahiers du Cinéma*)

Many of Berlin's defenders had followed their Führer's example and taken their own lives rather than go down fighting, putting a bullet through their brains after indulging in drunken orgies with their mistresses and comrades as the capital was engulfed in flames. They simply could not envisage a world in which they would no longer be the masters.

Similar scenes were being replayed across the country. A refugee from the East told the Hanover writer Ernst Jünger that during her journey across Germany she had looked into the living rooms of villas belonging to wealthy Prussian families and seen their lifeless bodies hunched around the dinner tables. They had killed themselves along with their entire families.

In a village in the north German region of Mecklenburg, a woman had shot 15 members of her family before drowning herself. In the midst of such collective madness, the death of the man who had set the whole tragedy in motion went largely unheeded.

The day Hitler shot himself, 19-year-old Erich Loest was hiding in a hayloft behind enemy lines with other boys of his 'Werwolf' unit. They were waiting anxiously with weapons at the ready for their first sight of American troops. Then the farmer came with news of the Führer's death and for a moment there was absolute silence, stillness. In an interview with German historian Malte Herwig, Erich said:

*Nothing of the kind ever entered my image of the world before. I was lying there, and then I heard life starting up again on the farm. A door slammed, a milk churn rattled. And I urgently needed a piss. So I got up and pissed down the roof beam. And that was life, in its primal form. I went on living.*

And so would millions of Germans, whether they had supported Hitler or not. Before this moment all that had been required of them was unquestioning obedience. In time they would have to acknowledge what they had been a part of, willing or otherwise. They had been bred to be leaders and now they were forced to face the fact that they were not only losers but members of a criminal regime reviled throughout the civilized world. What they had been conditioned to believe in was revealed to have been a lie. What they had been brought up to take pride in was now something to be ashamed of. But it was all they had known and for that reason many would resent being told that they ought to feel guilty. They simply hadn't known any better because they hadn't known anything else. From childhood, boys of Erich's age had been surrounded by the cult of the Führer. His earliest memory was of playing with a little tin Hitler, which raised its arm in the Nazi salute.

Günter Grass, the Nobel prize-winning novelist, became a symbol of Germany's moral conscience, but years later even he caught himself humming the Horst Wessel song, the anthem of the Nazi Party, while shaving. As Herwig rightly noted, for that generation it would never stop.

Until that fateful day in May 1945, German boys like Erich did not have to think – their superiors did that for them and the Führer, in turn, thought for all of them. Far in the future, Erich would grapple with his own ghosts and question the Nazi stereotypes. 'Some of the SA leaders in the city were very well respected and efficient people,' he recalled. His headmaster, for example, 'wasn't the fat brawling boozer … or the pub brawler of the Party's early years. He was correct, just Spartan.' And he would eventually make an uneasy peace with his past. Many others wouldn't even try. Or feel the need to do so.

Political scientist Iring Fetscher was 23 years old when the war ended and an artillery lieutenant serving in Poland with the Wehrmacht. After the war he converted to Catholicism, largely out of the need to confess, and wrote in *Curiosity and Fear*:

*It's all a long time ago now. But it's only forgotten, it hasn't passed away, it has just been repressed and lost – not overcome, not defeated … Yes, outside there is peace. If only it were inside us too!*

The German philosopher Karl Jaspers published *The Question of German Guilt*, a widely read pamphlet, just a year after the war ended, in which he said that the population did not care 'about the Judgment of history. All they want is for their suffering to cease.' That same year he gave a lecture in Heidelberg in which he told his audience:

*We did not go out on the streets when our Jewish friends were led away, nor did we cry out until they destroyed us as well. We preferred to stay alive on the weak, if justified, grounds that our deaths would not have helped in any case. That we stayed alive is our guilt.*

It was going to be different for all of them, but in May 1945 the primary concern was *überleben*, mere survival. They cast off their uniforms and discarded their party badges; they burned their membership cards and even destroyed their children's books and toys. Everything tainted with the tell-tale swastika or bearing Hitler's image had to go. The obligatory copy of *Mein Kampf*, which every loyal German had owned but few had read, was taken from pride of place on the mantlepiece where it could be seen and noted by visitors and thrown into the fire. Some chose to keep it – but only if toilet paper was scarce in their region.

Overnight the oath of loyalty to the Führer and the pledge of lifetime allegiance was forgotten, consigned to the past. But it was risky to clean the house out too soon. For three weeks after Hitler had ended it all, hardcore fanatics were still on the lookout for deserters and listening for defeatist talk. But to delay too long risked reprisals from the Allies, particularly the Russians.

## Identifying Hitler's remains

Marshal Zhukov, who led the battle for Berlin, had been entrusted with the capture of the German dictator and the rest of 'the Hitler Gang', but had to break the bad news to Stalin that the fate of the Führer was unknown, despite the official announcement of his death on German radio on 1 May, which claimed he had 'fallen while leading his troops in the defence of Berlin'. Confirmation of his suicide would not come for another month, but the charred remains of propaganda minister Goebbels had been found in a shell crater in the garden of the Reich Chancellery, along with his wife Magda. The bodies of their six children, whom she had poisoned, were found in the bunker.

The survivors from the Führer bunker, including Hitler's valet and secretaries, were seized and interrogated by Soviet military intelligence before being shipped off to Russia, where they spent much of the Cold War in Stalin's dreaded gulags and Soviet prisons. They made a brief return to Berlin in 1946 to show their

Adolf Hitler, pictured some ten days before his death as he inspects members of the Hitler Youth in the crazy hope they will defend Berlin for him and repel the Red Army.

captors where the fateful events had taken place, corroborating each other's testimonies to the satisfaction of the Soviets. The witnesses then confirmed that Hitler's body had been hastily, but only partly, cremated just yards from the bunker, together with that of his mistress Eva Braun. In the interim, the Soviets had located the dictator's remains and transported them to a Soviet military facility in Magdeburg, East Germany. Fragments of Hitler's jawbone and skull, complete with a bullet hole, were subsequently deposited in Moscow, after a formal identification had been made. The remainder of his body was said to have been burned, pulverized and scattered in the Biederitz river in the Soviet sector of Berlin.

## Evading capture

Some of the Nazi leadership had evaded capture.

Hitler's deputy and private secretary, Martin Bormann, was thought to have escaped on 1 May during a break-out from the bunker, until his bones were discovered decades later near the Lehrter railway bridge, a mile north of the Chancellery. He had bitten down on a cyanide capsule rather than be taken alive by the Russians.

*Reichsführer SS* Heinrich Himmler, whom Albert Speer had described as 'half schoolmaster, half crank', had been captured by the British near Lüneburg on 23 May. In a fruitless attempt to evade capture he had borrowed the uniform of a sergeant-major in the Secret Military Police (a branch of the Gestapo, which qualified him for immediate arrest), but was betrayed by another German POW, who resented having to do his chores. Rather than face the humiliation of a trial, he took his own life by swallowing cyanide. He would not be missed. The news of his earlier attempts to negotiate a surrender with the Allies had prompted many SS officers to commit suicide after they learned that the man who had sworn them to an oath of loyalty had betrayed them.

Speer, Field Marshal Keitel, General Alfred Jodl and some low-ranking Nazi ministers had joined Admiral Doenitz's sham 'government' in Flensburg, which lasted barely three weeks before the British arrested them all on 22 May. Both Himmler and Alfred Rosenberg, the Nazi 'philosopher', had implored Doenitz to give them a seat in his dummy cabinet and both had been rejected as liabilities. They had seriously believed that they would be allowed to govern the country after coming to an accommodation with the Allies.

Other notorious war criminals such as Adolf Eichmann and Dr Josef Mengele managed to slip through the net. Eichmann, who had organized the transportation of millions of Jews to the extermination camps, had been captured by the Americans, who believed he was just another bloodthirsty bureaucrat, or 'desk murderer', until he escaped and sailed for Argentina, where he was abducted by Mossad agents and taken to Israel for trial. Mengele and thousands of other minor Nazi functionaries were never caught and many of those who were apprehended managed to evade prosecution.

But there were enough familiar faces and notorious names in custody to answer for the crimes of the regime.

## Nazi symbols

The seizure of the Reichstag and the nearby Reich Chancellery, Hitler's headquarters, in Berlin was a priority for the Red Army, but they were not the only symbols of the regime that the Allies were eager to capture.

*The Reichstag*

Stalin had ordered nine divisions to storm the former German parliament building by 1 May so he could announce that Berlin had fallen during the annual May Day celebrations in Moscow. But 1,000 crack German troops were determined to hold out for as long as possible and made a desperate last stand. Fierce fighting was still taking place in the basement when the red flag was hoisted on the roof of the Reichstag at 10.30 on the night of 30 April by soldiers of the 756th regiment. It was too dark to take photographs of the historic moment, and so the event was restaged the next morning with different participants, who were honoured as heroes for the rest of their lives. The two men who had been first to raise the flag, Lt Koshkarbaev and Pte Bulatov, were pressured by the KGB to keep quiet and Bulatov subsequently committed suicide.

On the following morning the Russians entered the bombproof Führer bunker, eight and a half metres below the Chancellery, and found the last survivor, master mechanic Johannes Hentschel. He had stayed behind to maintain the electricity generators, the ventilation system and the water supply for the field hospital where the wounded were being treated. The bodies of those who had committed suicide were found where they had fallen, among them Generals Krebs and Burgdorf, while the rest of Hitler's inner circle had fled.

Hentschel was asleep when the first Soviet troops found him. They were women from a Red Army traffic unit, who helped

A staged photograph of Soviet troops raising the red flag over the Reichstag in Berlin: Stalin himself further rewrote history by falsely claiming that two Communist Party members were the soldiers who had done the daring deed. With that lie, he turned them into heroes of the Soviet Union.

themselves to clothes from the wardrobes of Eva Braun and Magda Goebbels. All of Hitler's personal papers had been burned on his orders and his study had been doused with petrol and set alight after his suicide, while the bodies of the six Goebbels children were found on their bunks and removed by the Russians for burial.

The Reich Chancellery was subsequently demolished, but the Führer bunker was allowed to remain until the late 1980s, when it was levelled. It now lies under a car park and housing complex and a single display board marks the place where Adolf Hitler ended his life. Marble panels which used to line the Chancellery reception halls were used in the rebuilding of the nearby Mohrenstrasse U-Bahn station.

Only two Nazi-era ministry buildings survive to this day – Goebbels' Propaganda Ministry HQ and Goering's Air Ministry building on Wilhelmstrasse, which now houses the German Finance Ministry.

## Tempelhof Airport

Tempelhof Airport also bears the symbols of the era in the form of huge stone imperial eagles with laurel wreaths in their claws, though they are missing the swastikas in the centre, the potent Nazi symbol which was banned after the war.

The airport was built by the Nazis in 1936 to provide an imposing entrance to the redesigned capital of Hitler's empire, to be named Germania. Its monumental terminal and empty corridors feature narrow floor to ceiling windows, from where a crowd of 100,000 could watch Luftwaffe flying displays and military parades.

But the terminal building was never finished. It only survives intact because the Allies knew they would need it after the war, which they did during the Berlin airlift that took place from 24 June 1948 to 1 May 1949. During that period nearly two and a half million tons of essential supplies were ferried in from Allied airbases in West Germany. On average a plane landed every minute, among them the 'candy bombers' bringing 20 tons of sweets for the city's children. Even bad weather couldn't stop the flights, which claimed the lives of 80 Allied airmen.

The airport's underground shelters still house the paintings designed to distract the city's children during air raids and there are also bullet holes from the fighting in April 1945.

*Gestapo headquarters*

Although the ominous and imposing building at 8 Prinz-Albrecht Strasse (now renamed Niederkirchnerstrasse) was not considered a strategic or significant target, its destruction by Allied bombing symbolized the end of the regime's reign of terror. The former HQ of the Gestapo was once the most dreaded address in Berlin. Victims were tortured and interrogated in the basement cells and in the offices on the upper floors the plans for the extermination of millions were made and administered by some 7,000 employees of the Nazi state, most of them young, ambitious university graduates. Of those 7,000, only 16 were to be prosecuted and just three were convicted.

The post-war German news magazine *Der Spiegel* named two: Erich Ehrlinger, a lawyer, who led a mobile murder squad in Ukraine, the feared 1b *Einsatzkommando*, and Josef Spacil, a Munich businessman and SS department head. Ehrlinger was excused trial on medical grounds and yet he lived another 35 years, while Spacil appeared as a witness at Nuremberg, for which he appeared to have received immunity from prosecution.

The building's 39 cells had housed communists, church officials, trade unionists and members of the various socialist parties who opposed the party in the early years, as well as members of the Red Orchestra resistance group and those German officers accused of participating in the 20 July plot against Hitler. Among them were Pastor Martin Niemoller, Erich Honecker, future leader of the GDR, and the Social Democrat Kurt Schumacher. In all, some 15,000 individuals were taken there, of whom very few were permitted to leave.

The SS had their headquarters in the adjacent Prinz-Albrecht Hotel and the SS Intelligence Service, the SD, were housed in Prinz-Albrecht-Palais in nearby Wilhelmstrasse.

It is now the site of a museum and documentation centre dedicated to recording the crimes of the dictatorship.

## The Eagle's Nest

In the last weeks of the war, the Allies were expecting to have to make a costly assault on Hitler's alpine redoubt, overlooking the town of Berchtesgaden in the Obersalzberg. Here the Nazi leadership had built luxury private villas to be near their Führer, who had chosen the site for his private summer residence, the Berghof, a luxury chalet that he had purchased with the royalties from the sales of *Mein Kampf* and had subsequently enlarged at considerable expense. It was here that he had planned the invasion of Poland and received foreign dignitaries, among them the Duke and Duchess of

Windsor, his Axis ally Benito Mussolini and the British prime minister Neville Chamberlain, who came to sign the infamous Munich agreement guaranteeing 'peace in our time'.

It was believed that the Bavarian retreat would be the site of the Nazis' last stand. To add substance to the rumours, a fortified stronghold had been created, which contained an SS barracks and a 3,000-metre-long network of bombproof tunnels hewn out of the mountain. Within the tunnels were 70 rooms, offices, living quarters and Martin Bormann's banqueting hall. More than 40 farms and private homes had been commandeered to build it, on a site spread over 650 acres, but Hitler had decided

Something to show the folks back home: victorious US soldiers are photographed in front of Hitler's Eagle's Nest in a set-up shot for *Life* magazine.

to remain in Berlin and the complex had long been abandoned. Events revealed that the idea of the Nazis' last stand in the Alps had been nothing but a myth.

A massive bombing raid by British Lancaster bombers in April 1945 destroyed many of the villas and damaged the Berghof, but much of it was still standing when the Americans arrived a month later. The US 3rd Infantry Division took it on 4 May without a shot being fired and immediately began the celebrations by raiding the wine cellar and pocketing prized Nazi artefacts for shipping home to the United States.

High above the Berghof and accessible by a private underground lift is the Eagle's Nest, a conference and banqueting centre built as a birthday present for Hitler by his fawning acolyte Martin Bormann. Perched on the summit, 6,000 feet above sea level, it offered a spectacular view of the Bavarian Alps and on a clear day the Führer could see Salzburg, Mozart's birthplace, in the distance.

The Eagle's Nest was, however, rarely used. One notable occasion was the wedding of Eva Braun's sister Gretl to SS officer Hermann Fegelein on 3 June 1944. Less than a year later, Hitler had his brother-in-law shot for desertion.

*The Brown House*

Munich was the birthplace of National Socialism, the scene of the failed putsch of 1923 and the location of the NSDAP headquarters, known as the Brown House. The 100-year-old neoclassical villa at the Königsplatz was bought by the party in 1930 and extensively renovated by Hitler's architect, Paul Ludwig Troost. Its amenities included a private lift from the underground garage to Goering's apartment, so that prominent business associates could visit in secret.

It was derided by the democratic press, who called it the Delusions of Grandeur Palace. Hitler and his deputy Rudolf Hess had their offices there, as did the SS until Hitler's succession to the chancellorship in 1933, when the party relocated to Berlin. Badly damaged in an Allied air raid in 1943, Munich was completely destroyed in early 1945.

The undefended city was taken by the Americans on 30 April, which was the day after they had liberated Dachau on the outskirts of the city and the day on which Hitler killed himself.

At the head of the US reconnaissance unit was 27-year-old Hamburg-born Wolfgang Robinow, who had been hoping to join the Hitler Youth until he learned that he had four Jewish grandparents. He was then forced to leave the country of his birth but was able to return to see the end of the regime that had rejected him. Ironically, his application to join the US Air Force was also denied, but on the grounds that he was German. He was later recruited by the US Army, who needed fluent German speakers to interrogate prisoners. Among them was Leni Riefenstahl, director of the Nazi propaganda film *Triumph of the Will* (because Robinow's commanding officer wanted her autograph), and a Gestapo officer who admitted that he had no idea how many people he had murdered. 'Are you in the habit of counting how many slices of bread you have for breakfast in a year?' was all he would say.

At Marienplatz in the centre of the city, where Hitler had been photographed in a crowd cheering the announcement of war in August 1914, Robinow found an unexpected welcome.

*We were greeted as the great liberators of the
city, which, to be honest, really made me angry
at the time. This was, after all, the capital of the
movement. It was where the Nazi party got its start
and where its main propaganda organ the newspaper
the* Völkischer Beobachter *was headquartered.
And they were now happy to be 'liberated?'*

Robinow then marched over to Munich police headquarters
where he was saluted by the Nazis, who presented him with
their weapons, each labelled with their owner's name and the
serial number of the pistol.

*Nuremberg*

In contrast to the capture of Munich, the US Army was forced
to fight for every foot of ground in Nuremberg, the medieval
city which had been the setting for the annual Nazi Party rallies
in the pre-war years.

The US 7th Army fought an intense and costly five-day,
house-to-house battle for the city from 16 April 1945, at the
end of which 90 per cent of the picturesque fairy tale city was
nothing but rubble, broken glass and twisted metal.

Hitler had ordered the city to be defended to the last
man, but under heavy artillery bombardment and repeated
air attacks the final defenders were eventually forced to
surrender. It was a bitter blow to fading German morale.

The local Gauleiter (district leader), Karl Holz, had
assured Hitler that he would not surrender the city and
died after rejecting repeated pleas to capitulate. He had

killed the mayor, who had wanted to concede defeat.

*My Führer: The final struggle for the town of the party has begun. The soldiers are fighting bravely, and the population is proud and strong. I shall remain in this most German of all towns to fight and to die. In these hours my heart beats more than ever in love and faith for the wonderful German Reich and its people. The National Socialist idea shall win and conquer all diabolic schemes. Greetings from the National Socialists of the Gau Franconia who are faithful to Germany.*

American troops march through the ruins of Nuremberg. They met with incredibly fierce resistance after the German army decided to fight to the last man in April 1945.

Some of the fiercest fighting was around the rally grounds, the Luitpold Arena and the Zeppelin Field, which had been the scene of massed rallies of the party faithful. But these sites had been built in haste and using shoddy materials, which resulted in their severe deterioration over the years. Hitler had commissioned Albert Speer, his architect and later his armaments minister, to design monumental buildings that would make imposing ruins in the coming millennia, but within a decade these had either been completely destroyed or had deteriorated to such a degree that in many cases only the foundations remained.

One of the few buildings in Nuremberg that could be repaired in a short time was the Palace of Justice, where the trials of the major war criminals would be held throughout the following winter.

## Getting back on their feet

US intelligence officer Peter Sichel recalled his impression of returning to the country of his birth shortly after the surrender.

*It was like Armageddon, it really was. It was horrific. Everybody was so worn out, so depressed, so poor, so lacking in food, so lacking in any hope. We thought it was very possible that the Nazis had a plan to have guerrillas after the war to make our lives difficult and we expected something. We found when we got there, there was nothing. There was no resistance. No sign of it whatsoever. The conditions weren't there for anybody to resist. And I don't think the will was there to resist. This was a total collapse and everybody accepted it.*

Many German people felt an urgency to return to normality as soon as possible and in doing so to put the past behind them. The capital's streets were cleared of rubble and made passable within a fortnight of the last shot being fired and the buses, trams and the U-Bahn began operating a limited service. This was essential, because all private transport had been requisitioned, even bicycles. The S-Bahn (rapid transit railway) was operational by the end of the month.

On every street were plastered countless notices pleading desperately for news of loved ones: *'Iche suche meine Frau'*, *'Ich suche meinen Mann'* ('I'm searching for my wife' or 'my husband'). It seemed that everyone was looking for someone they had lost or had been parted from. Practically every wall, telephone pole and tree trunk was covered with these pleas. As Lieutenant Colonel Byford-Jones wrote:

*On the trees that flanked the pavements were many thousands of little cards and envelopes bearing desperate messages in pencil, ink, or typescript, some embellished with a crude drawing, asking people to change luxury articles for something that could be eaten or worn, or appealing for work of any kind, or offering marriage, companionship and more doubtful liaison. Everywhere there were these pathetic appeals, literally tens upon tens of thousands of them, and around each tree from early morning until late at night crowds gathered, making notes.*

But it was all taking place in a surreal landscape littered with burned-out tanks, abandoned anti-aircraft guns, shallow graves at the side of the road and buildings without exterior walls – the '*Sperlings-Lust*' (or 'Sparrow's Delight'), so called because the inhabitants might find themselves falling through the air if the unstable structures collapsed.

It wasn't only the landscape that had been altered. The cities were eerily quiet and that was equally unnerving. British intelligence officer and interpreter George Clare, an Austrian by birth, had lived in Berlin before the war and was struck by the uncanny silence on his return in January 1946.

'Berlin had assaulted one's ears with lively and strident crescendos, harsh atonal, high-decibel: a medley of blaring car horns, squeaking brakes, snorting buses, clanging trams, shouting newspaper sellers.' Now the only sounds were 'wooden-soled footsteps, the rattle of a handcart or an occasional tram, the chugging of a wood-fuelled bus, the gear-clash of an allied army lorry. This absence of the constant roar of city life was more unsettling than the sight of bombed and shelled buildings.'

The absence of men his own age was another rather disconcerting sight.

*... the men were mostly old or elderly, bowed and bitter-faced; the few youngish ones who were about – emaciated shadows of the soldiers who had almost conquered an entire continent – looked pathetic and downtrodden in the tattered remnants of their Wehrmacht uniforms. The women were of all ages and, with so many men killed and hundreds*

*of thousands in prisoner-of-war camps, they, not as*
*formerly the Prussian male, dominated the scene.*

The National Socialist experiment had failed. It had been
defeated militarily and it had also been revealed to be
ideologically bankrupt. Even if the ordinary German civilians
didn't care to think about the lies and deceitful slogans with
which they had been bombarded since 1933, they might have
allowed themselves a moment to appreciate the cruel irony
of their current situation. The Nazi idyll, which had confined
the woman's role to '*Kinder, Küche, Kirche*' (children, kitchen,
church), had been overturned. Now it was the women who
were the breadwinners, both literarily and figuratively. They
foraged for food and fuel and did whatever was necessary to
survive while their men lay idle, shell-shocked and dependent
on their women to provide. Those men who did find work were
often poorly paid and relied on their wives and daughters to
supplement their income.

The romanticized image of women as the self-sacrificing
heart of the Aryan family, which the Nazis had projected as
the ideal, was now reality, but under dramatically different
circumstances. While their men were away fighting, the
women had been working in the factories, on the land and
in administration, despite Hitler's assertion that National
Socialism would be 'an entirely male event' and in spite of
the regime having barred women from politics, public life,
the professions and higher education. Even though they were
living under one of the most repressive regimes in modern
times, the women of Germany had become, in the main,

self-reliant, resourceful and forcefully assertive. According to British historian Richard Bessel:

*Men having been indoctrinated to feel like 'supermen' were, in varying degrees, unable to deal in a dignified manner with the occupation forces in the role of subordinates, often discrediting themselves in the eyes of their wives through awkward obsequiousness.*

The refugees fared no better in the DP (displaced persons) camps according to F. Donovan, a British Military Government official.

*The actuality of conditions in the centres fell sadly short of the hopes and excitement that had filled [the DPs] when they knew the war was over and they had been liberated ... displaced persons were frequently worse off than they had been under the Nazis.*

Kathryn Hulme, a director of one of the camps in the American zone, wrote home:

*It is hard to believe that some shining tins of meat paste and sardines could almost start a riot ... that bags of Lipton's tea and tins of [instant] coffee and bars of vitaminised chocolate could drive men almost insane with desire ... This is as much a part of the destruction of Europe as are the gaunt ruins of Frankfurt. Only this is the ruin of the human soul. It is a thousand times more painful to see.*

Unfortunately, the DPs did not always behave in the way their liberators expected. Not all of them were grateful and willing to obey orders or form orderly queues for medical checks, disinfection and registration. Many gave vent to a long pent-up desire for revenge and ran riot. In Hanover, hundreds of Russian DPs besieged the town hall, breaking into the wine cellars and smashing vats of wine and spirits. The floor was soon six inches deep in a heady alcoholic mixture and several of the rioters drowned after becoming intoxicated.

The DPs soon became a convenient scapegoat for the general lawlessness that abounded. However, the increasing crime rate was not substantiated by the number of criminal convictions. By the spring of 1947, seven million DPs had returned to their own countries, leaving just one million in Germany. Many of these were in camps rather than wandering around the country creating havoc.

John Hynd (centre in hat), British zone administrator, talks to refugees in Berlin waiting for transport to take them to their homes in the West, December 1945.

# A question of sympathy

In a private letter to his wife, British documentary filmmaker Humphrey Jennings wrote:

*They certainly don't behave guilty or beaten. They have their old fatalism to fall back on: 'Kaput' says the housewife finding the street water pipe not working ... and then looks down the streets and says 'Kaput ... alles ist kaput.' Everything ... how right – but absolutely no suggestion that it might be their fault – her fault. 'Why' asks another woman fetching water 'why do not you help us?' 'You' being us. At the same time nothing is clearer straight away than that we cannot – must not – leave them to stew in their own juice ...*

For all their altruistic ideals and Christian missionary compassion, the British were, at that time, not naturally sympathetic towards the Germans. Even highly educated and empathic individuals such as Jennings could not contain their innate dislike for the German people. At the end of his tour of the country, during which he had filmed the acclaimed documentary *A Defeated People*, Jennings wrote to his wife, describing them as:

*... terrified, rabbit-eyed, over-willing, too friendly, without an inch of what we call character among a thousand ... almost every attribute that we strive to make grow, cultivate, has been bred or burnt out of them, exiled, thrown into gas-chambers, frightened, until you have a*

*nation of near zombies with all the parts of human beings but really no soul – no oneness of personality to hold the parts together and shine out of the eyes ... Yes they can laugh and cry and do almost everything that so called normal humans can and do – yet there is something missing – helpless now, untrustful of anything, most of all themselves – precisely not 'The Triumph of the Will'.*

The British troops had been warned to regard the population with suspicion and treat them as a wounded adversary who might turn on them as soon as they lowered their guard. In *The British Soldier's Pocket Book*, issued to all British troops on entering Germany, the Tommy was urged to suppress any feelings of pity.

*You will see much suffering in Germany and much to awake your pity. You may also find that many Germans, on the surface at least, seem pleasant enough and that they will even try to welcome you as friends ... The Germans have much to unlearn [and] much to atone for ... The German people as a whole cannot escape a large share of responsibility ... it is only by the sacrifice of thousands upon thousands of your fellow countrymen and Allies, and at a cost of untold suffering at home and abroad through five long years, that British troops are at last on German soil. Think first of all this when you are tempted to sympathise with those who today are reaping the fruits of their policy, both in peace and war.*

It continued:

*You may see many pitiful sights. Hard luck stories
may somehow reach you. Some of them may be
true, at least in part, but most will be hypocritical
attempts to win sympathy ... SO BE ON YOUR
GUARD AGAINST 'PROPAGANDA' IN THE FORM OF
HARD LUCK STORIES. Be fair and just, but don't
be soft ... THERE WILL BE NO BRUTALITY ABOUT
A BRITISH OCCUPATION, BUT NEITHER WILL
THERE BE SOFTNESS OR SENTIMENTALITY.*

In issue 2 of the *British Zone Review* in October 1945, a letter
from Subaltern Lucia Lawson began a heated debate among the
servicemen and women as to how to respond to the deprivations.

*You will say that those sweet little children with curly fair
hair and blue eyes are all potential killers, but with their
spindly legs and lips just turning blue from lack of food
it is hardly in human nature to hate them. The old man
and woman who I saw digging for tree roots in the ruins
of the Tiergarten for food, surely deserve a little pity, or
do they? The young girl dressed in a thin summer frock
who I found sleeping under the shelter of a pile of rubble
in the Kaiser Wilhelm church, is she to be hated too?
Hundreds are now dying from starvation and disease. In
a couple of months the number may easily be doubled.*

It brought several responses. Flight Lieutenant E.A. Salmon identified the dilemma:

*If we appear sorry for their plight, they will only too readily assume the role of martyrdom. If we are harsh and indifferent they will accept us as conquerors and wait for revenge, instead of learning the meaning of civilized conduct, which must be our ultimate aim to teach.*

To which others responded:

*Do not let us be deceived by some cases of sufferings, which, painful as they may be, constitute only a fraction of the misery the Germans have brought about all over the world. (F. Royen, Berlin, November)*

*Our mission is to show the Germans they failed because they ignored the principles of humanity. We must punish the criminals responsible and teach the others by example that we have something better to offer. (Sergeant J.P. Noonan, November)*

*If I were in Yugoslavia, the children there should have all my chocolate and the German children none. But I'm not in Yugoslavia. ... Sooner than see kindness in the wrong place, some people would see no kindness at all. (D.G. Hannover, December)*

# Montgomery – a military operation

*The detachments entered into a land of desolation
and bewilderment. Government above the level of
the Parish Council had ceased. Everything was in
disorder, people were stunned and helpless.*
General Brian Robertson,
British Army of Occupation, January 1946

Various directives had been issued by the War Office in London
in October 1944 to enable the British to organize the restoration
of basic facilities and establish an interim administration, but
these were found to be inadequate or impractical due to the sheer
scale of the devastation and the collapse of the administrative
infrastructure.

In May 1945, Field Marshal Montgomery, commander-in-
chief and governor of the British zone, admitted that he had
received no training to help him cope with the situation and
was conscious that it was a matter of urgency if anarchy was
to be avoided. He decided that the only way he could establish
order was to treat the situation as if it was a military campaign
and wage a war against the elements, disorder and the chronic
shortages which threatened to undermine Allied efforts to 'win
the peace', as he termed it.

First of all, he empowered army 'Civil Affairs' detachments
to take control of all aspects of civil administration and be
responsible for the needs of the general population, thereby
ensuring that former Nazis were excluded from local politics.
Power devolved to the regions, new political parties were

licensed and free elections were held in October 1946 to select representatives at local, regional and zonal level.

Montgomery also ordered the release of more than a million German POWs to work in the fields and the coal mines, relieving a substantial number of British troops of the responsibility of guarding men who would otherwise be idle. Restoring the mines was only partially successful, though, as there were simply not enough men to produce sufficient coal – only 30,000 agreed to work in the mines – and nor were there adequate raw materials to get German industry in the British zone back to pre-war levels, with the result that the British government had to subsidize the German economy to

German POWs chalk the graffiti of happy anticipation on a train taking them home from British camps in 1948. This image featured in a piece for *Picture Post* cheerfully entitled 'The German Prisoners Arrive in Civvy Street'.

the tune of £80 million during the first year of the occupation. It was largely due to British efforts that the transport system in the British zone was restored, that basic services were provided (albeit at a subsistence level) and that some industrial plants were up and running again (Volkswagen being a prime example, with German workers encouraged to take active control of production and being given incentives to increase output).

At first there was considerable resentment at the preferential treatment demanded by the Allies, particularly regarding accommodation – at a time of great housing shortage – and transport facilities, for which the occupation forces were given priority. There were initially numerous strikes, protests and demonstrations, but in time these became less frequent and the presence of the British and the Americans was gradually seen as being beneficial, particularly with regard to preserving the peace during the Cold War.

## Order from chaos

Field Marshal Montgomery's deputy Brian Robertson, who would succeed 'Monty' as military governor of the British sector, admitted that both he and his fellow officers were totally unprepared for the role which was suddenly thrust upon them. Few spoke German – Robertson had never even been to Germany – and yet they were now in charge of 20 million people living in an area half the size of Britain, who were looking to them to provide leadership, stability and, most urgently, the basics for sustaining life. Robertson had been given no forewarning of his appointment and had taken no part in the preparatory discussion and plans for the British administration of post-war Germany. 'I knew nothing about the situation at all. Nothing.' It was not an impediment, as it turned out, as the politicians back in London knew even less.

As Christopher Knowles observed in *Winning the Peace*:

*Plans prepared during the war had assumed, incorrectly, that a central German administration would remain in place. The main task of the occupation forces and the Civilian Control Commission were expected to be to prevent armed resistance, which never materialized, and to supervise and control German authorities, rather than having to act as civilian administrators themselves, maintain law and order and undertake reconstruction work ...*

Nevertheless, Montgomery and his men believed that it was incumbent upon them to learn how to do this and do it to the very best of their ability.

Robertson compared the process they faced to that of a policeman who is on hand to take charge of the scene of an accident. He did not have to be an expert, but he saw clearly what needed to be done. As Robertson wrote in the *British Zone Review*:

*The German apple cart has been upset, the madmen who were in charge of it are dead or in prison, the German people lies bleeding and helpless. We represent the policemen destined to take charge of the proceedings.*

The understated, pragmatic approach of the British to the problem of post-war Germany was encapsulated in an article that appeared in the first issue of the *British Zone Review*, published in September 1945.

*When the British 213 Military Detachment took over the Nazi-run town on May 10, Buxtehude was like a clock with its spring unwound. There was no gas, and there was no electricity. The water was impure. The town's small industries were at a standstill. The flour mills were idle. Road transport had stopped, and no trains ran. Today the Nazi bosses are gone, and the town has a Burgomeister, a Social Democrat, who was three times imprisoned by them. The public services have been restored. Trains are running, and there is a daily bus for those who have passes to say that their journeys are really necessary ... How have these things happened?*

*'It has just been part of the drill for dealing with such problems,' a British Army officer of the Military Government Detachment told me. 'The German people have been obedient and cooperative. We have told them what they must do and they have got on with the job.'*

## Art and industry plundered

Curiously, the Russians had a very different set of priorities. They put the restoration of culture at the top of their list. Consequently, an Academy of Creative Arts was founded during the first month of the peace and by the winter the first exhibition was opened, its theme being 'Modern French Painting'. It was the first attempt to denazify the nation by encouraging ordinary Germans to appreciate what the Nazis had condemned as 'degenerate art'. This was swiftly followed by other exhibitions, some of them furnished with art confiscated by the regime. But while the Russians were publicly seducing the population with edifying art, they were quietly dismantling much of the country's industry and shipping it back to Mother Russia.

The Russians also sent around two and a half million works of art back to the Soviet Union while their allies rescued what they could under the pretext of holding it in trust for the German people. Although no one was fooled by this, there was a case to be made for transporting precious works of art to safety as so many had been destroyed during the fighting and more would be vandalized by thoughtless soldiers, who used statues for target practice and defaced paintings out of sheer boredom.

Power, telephones and the postal service were not restored until the summer and even then they were erratic, but at least German towns and cities were beginning to see a semblance of normality. Financial, cultural and sports organizations were established, incentives were offered to those Germans starting essential businesses and necessary supplies to both large and small food producers, from factories to family bakeries, were given priority. Soup kitchens were set up, mobile canteens toured the cities and graded ration cards were issued, with workers being given precedence over former Nazis, who were allocated the lowest, subsistence

Mathilde Ludendorff, wife of the famous general who died in 1937, was an eccentric psychiatrist with *Völkisch* (populist and racist) beliefs. She continued to express her anti-Semitic opinions after the war and was tried before a denazification tribunal (or *Spruchkammer*) in 1949 and found guilty.

ration. It would benefit no one to prolong the agony and the privations.

As a cabinet minute to the British Foreign Office in autumn 1945 put it succinctly: 'Unless we do what we can to help, we may lose next winter what we won at such terrible cost last spring.'

And while the population scavenged for scraps, members of the Allied Control Commission satiated themselves at nightly banquets that would have fed an entire district.

As Lieutenant Colonel Byford-Jones wrote in *Berlin Twilight*:

*... each meeting of the Council was followed by a banquet such as few emperors can ever have improved upon when entertaining visiting Royalty. ... This small body*

*of men, most of whom had seen or known the worst of human suffering and deprivation on the world's worst battlefields in the bloody years, then sat down for an hour in a ruined city of over three million souls, all of whom were learning in hunger and poverty the high cost of aggression, and ate the choicest of food and drank the finest of wines the needy could produce.*

Nazi resistance activist Ruth Andreas-Friedrich kept a diary of life during and after the dictatorship, in which small details reveal the depth to which the once proud nation had fallen. On 11 September 1946 she wrote:

*The areas around the Allied officers' mess halls abound with trophy hunters. Catch, they think, and take home the cans that have been thrown away, to scrape them out, lick them clean or wash the remains with water into their soup. Catch! If you are hungry enough it doesn't disgust you. In the years since the war, thousands who 'once knew better days' have ceased feeling disgusted.*

Occasionally the ignorance of the Allies in regard to local customs and culture proved disastrous in the war for winning hearts and minds. The American administrators of the Marshall Plan, an initiative to help Germans help themselves, made a grave error in sending corn to the hungry citizens of Bavaria, where corn was traditionally fed to pigs. The Bavarians took it as an insult and have resented the Americans ever since.

## Post-war German politics

Harold Ingrams, a former colonial official who had been made head of Administration and Local Government (a subsidiary of the Control Commission), believed that German politics had to be decentralized to prevent a revival of National Socialism. As he observed: 'The parish council does not go to war.' But his attempts to impose a British electoral system on the British zone were met with hostility. The Germans resisted all attempts to persuade them to adopt the British 'first past the post' system and also rejected the imposition of unpaid representatives on local councils to replace their elected *Bürgermeister* or mayors. They contended that prior to the dictatorship Germany had enjoyed a strong, workable democratic tradition and they demanded that they be given the chance to prove it could work just as effectively in the post-war years.

## The black market

*Every man, woman and child in Western Europe was engaged to a greater or lesser degree in illegal trading of one kind or another. In fact, it [was] hardly possible to support existence without so doing.*
Lt Gen. Frederick Morgan

The black market was not something the occupation forces could readily locate, control or clamp down on. It could spring up anywhere where people saw an opportunity to trade what they could spare for the items they were desperately in need of. Even the presence of military police proved no deterrent.

Lieutenant Wladimir Gelfand, commander of a Soviet mortar platoon, was in the habit of visiting Berlin's Alexanderplatz, where a thriving black market offered everything that was in scarce supply elsewhere. One morning, however, he was dismayed to find Red Army MPs patrolling the square and demanding to see everyone's papers, even those of their senior officers. Being a resourceful man, he had the bright idea to have his shoes polished at one of several shoe-shine stands and waited until his presence attracted a crowd.

'I was immediately surrounded by people who started offering me goods that they had hidden underneath their coats.'

The crowd was dispersed repeatedly by the MPs, who couldn't find anything amiss. Meanwhile, Gelfand had managed to buy a leather jacket, a shirt, several pairs of socks and a pair of gloves.

Those who had nothing left to barter were often tempted to offer themselves in exchange for food, coal and other essentials and it wasn't only the women. So many women and young girls had been raped repeatedly by Soviet troops that they must have felt that in choosing to sell themselves they were at least doing it of their own free will.

German refugee Ursula Gray recalled: 'A piece of soap was your most valuable possession. I know some very fine people who would do anything for soap. And you lose some of your human dignity when you are so hungry, without food, without clothing, without anything.'

In contrast, soldiers of the occupying armies had much to barter with. Many had pocketed lighters, watches and other personal valuables from their dead enemies without a second thought. As far as they were concerned, such trifles were there for the taking and their previous owners would have no further need of them. They must also have felt that they had a certain right to compensate themselves for the risks they had taken and the privations they had endured. It was the unwritten law of war – to the victor go the spoils.

And although these items were frequently exchanged with their comrades, they also had access to commodities which were in demand by the general population, namely cigarettes, coffee, alcohol and chocolate. With the Reichsmark now worthless, these commonplace items became the new currency.

A hairdryer for a pair of shiny shoes: two women trade off at the official barter market in West Berlin introduced by the Allies in a futile attempt to stem the tide of black markets after the war when the necessities of life were in short supply.

A soldier could have his laundry done for ten cigarettes a week and cigarettes were to be had cheaply from the stores and the officers' mess, while chocolate and other items could be legitimately obtained from the Red Cross clubs, the NAAFI and its American equivalent the PX (the Post Exchange). They had little else to spend their money on and little incentive to pay when so much could be had for the asking.

With the destruction of so many factories, shops and other places of employment, the majority of Germans had no source of income. Those who were willing to swallow their pride and make the best of it found employment as cooks, cleaners and waiters in Allied camp canteens, while others acted as secretaries and translators for the 'Amis'.

A fortunate few filled the posts vacated by minor Allied officials, provided they were well educated and prepared to accept lower wages than the British and American personnel whom they had replaced. Each job had its own dubious 'perks'. For instance, waiters could add a few dollars to their earnings by salvaging cigarette butts from the ashtrays and selling them on. As one young American soldier remarked in *The New Republic*, a stateside magazine, he and his buddies were free from parental supervision, plied with more money than they knew what to do with, granted power over women equal to that of movie stars and let loose 'among a people who had lost all moral standards'.

German children soon found working the black market more exciting than stealing coal and it was considerably less dangerous. Eleven-year-old Peter Lauden and his friends viewed it as a game, a means of extorting money from adults, and boasted about their 'heroic deeds on the battlefield of the black market', while Allied welfare organizations portrayed them as little criminals with no regard for the law and as moral degenerates. It is true that some progressed to a life of serious crime and a number of the girls became prostitutes and drug addicts as a result of their youthful activities, but the majority of that generation thought of themselves as resourceful. They were simply doing what was needed to get through another day.

The Allied authorities managed to persuade the reluctant and undermanned German police to stage periodic campaigns against black marketeers using British, French or American soldiers to enforce the law, but mounting an operation was time-consuming and was considered a waste of manpower and resources. Besides, there was no consensus about what constituted a serious offence and even when arrests were made the German civil courts were unable to deal with the accused. Conversely, the incentive to profit from exploiting the dire need of the civilian population was often so great that previously law-abiding soldiers and officials were tempted to turn a blind eye to such activities in exchange for a bribe. Others actively participated in supplying or facilitating the black market in the belief that it didn't harm anyone, so great was the profusion of surplus liquor and other goods that could be purloined without fear of arrest or discovery.

But there were limits. Such easy profits led some soldiers to blur the line between minor infractions of the regulations and wholesale crime. At least one British soldier was executed for involvement in a murder directly related to his black market activities and countless others were court-martialled or disciplined for lesser offences.

It was not until 1948, when the German mark was introduced as the new currency of West Germany, that the economy picked up practically overnight and the black market went out of business. In addition, every citizen was given 40 Deutschmarks to start a new life by the new West German government. However, as a consequence there was a marked disparity in the standard of living between those working in East and West Germany, which only seemed to widen with the years.

*The people are absolutely without history in every respect ... The Third Reich is already as good as forgotten, everyone had been opposed to it, had always been opposed to it.*
Victor Klemperer, diarist, 11 May 1945

## Collective guilt

*We could see the physical destruction, but the effect of vast economic disruption, and political, social and psychological destruction ... completely escaped us.*
Dean Acheson, US Under Secretary of State, 1947

Germany was now occupied by its former enemies, who were warned that they should neither fraternize with civilians nor trust them or sympathize with them. Not even the children should be approached, because they might have been in uniform only weeks before and armed with the Panzerfaust, a portable anti-tank rocket. Girls as young as eight had been trained to use the weapon and it would not be easy to convince a generation indoctrinated with the malign ideology of National Socialism that Hitler and the Nazi leadership had brought this misery on their own people.

Hitler, Himmler and Goebbels had committed suicide rather than fall into the hands of their enemies, while other members of the 'Hitler Gang', such as Goering, Ribbentrop and Doenitz, had been taken into custody and were awaiting indictment on charges of war crimes in the cells at Nuremberg. The trials would reveal the full extent of Nazi atrocities, including the plan to exterminate millions by implementing the 'Final Solution to the Jewish Question', as Hitler's executioners termed the genocide of Europe's Jewish population.

To the victors it had been a costly but necessary war against tyranny. Good against evil. But convincing ordinary Germans that they had been complicit in the crimes of one of the most odious and murderous regimes of modern times would be extremely difficult – and some would argue that it was also undesirable. Forcing a defeated, starving and resentful population to accept the concept of collective guilt would have to take second place to providing them with food, water, medicine and shelter.

Screenings of newsreels showing Nazi atrocities did not have the desired effect.

The poet and broadcaster Stephan Hermlin went to one of the few cinemas that were still open in Frankfurt and saw that most of the audience turned away and did not look back until it was over. 'That turned away face is the attitude of many millions,' he wrote. It is all the more worrying when one knows that they only attended because it was compulsory, a condition of their being awarded their ration cards.

Hitler Youth leader Alfons Heck came to view these atrocity films with indifference.

*The mountains of emaciated corpses had the opposite effect from what our conquerors intended. We thought they were fakes, posed to indict all Germans. The French became so incensed by our indifference that they rammed us with rifle butts. It was some time before I could accept the truth of the Holocaust, nearly three decades more before I could write or speak about German guilt and responsibility.*

Hans Hebe, a German émigré who returned to establish newspapers in the American sector, noted: 'The idea that the nation should look back, questioning and repenting ... [is] the concept of a conqueror.'

The films had a very different impact in the occupied countries. In Poland 15-year-old Janina David sat with clenched teeth through a screening of the Soviet documentary on the liberation of Majdanek, while other members of the audience wept and prayed. Some fainted. It had destroyed her 'last childish dream; there was no God.'

However, one initiative to re-educate former members of the Hitler Youth was successful, because it simply offered German youth a similar programme of activities to those enjoyed by adolescents in America. Its mix of outdoor activities with informal discussions about democracy and dictatorship allowed a free and frank exchange of views during which many former Nazis came to appreciate to what extent they had been indoctrinated by their former leaders.

It was the view of many that the Germans were largely unrepentant and sorry only that they had lost the war. British intelligence officer George Clare found his former countrymen's 'constant whingeing' and 'inexhaustible self-pity' sickening and in stark contrast to how 'pitiless they were in victory'.

The US secretary of the treasury, Henry Morgenthau, had advocated dividing Germany between the victors, dismantling its industry and turning the entire country over to agriculture so that it would never again have the capacity for re-armament. It was a policy which at one time had the support of Roosevelt and Churchill, but by 1943 they had both come to realize that it was economically unviable. Europe could only recover from the war if it could utilize German industry, especially the plants in the Ruhr. A divided Germany would require policing and the Allies did not have the resources to provide long-term patrols and monitoring.

Proving to the Germans that the army of occupation was in fact an army of liberation, which had freed them from an oppressive dictatorship, could only be achieved by assisting with reconstruction and showing some measure of compassion, not by gutting the country of its assets and certainly not by damning them all by association.

Retribution would have to wait and when it came it would have to be directed at those personally responsible for having brought about the suffering and destruction.

# Chapter Two

# JUSTICE AND RETRIBUTION

*You can have vengeance or peace,*
*but you can't have both.*
Former US President Herbert Hoover, 1946

## Manhunt – the hunt for Nazi war criminals

In the last months of the war in Europe, the Nazi leadership ordered the destruction of the extermination camps and the liquidation of all surviving witnesses in a desperate attempt to erase the evidence of their abominable crimes. In some instances, they attempted to conceal the existence of the camps by erecting houses on the sites and installing locals who would claim they had been farming the land for decades. At the same time, some of the most notorious mass murderers in history escaped across the 'rat lines' to South America, some aided by sympathetic officials in the Vatican. Others simply melted into the population and hoped that their past would not catch up with them.

Meanwhile, both superpowers recruited Nazi scientists and technicians for their rival space programmes, disregarding their roles in the deaths of the thousands of slave labourers who had built the facilities and worked in the factories producing Hitler's secret weapons. Within a year, the will of the two superpowers to prosecute their former enemies appeared to have waned, as they squared up to each other in a new conflict, the Cold War. Justice, it seemed, was not only blind but quick to forget when the world faced the threat of nuclear war.

But there were those who had seen and suffered too much to forgive or forget. They would not rest until the murderers had been brought to account, despite the dangers, the threats and intimidation, public apathy and the bureaucracy of government authorities who appeared to have something to hide.

## Bergen-Belsen trials

Lucie Adelsberger, Jewish prisoner and physician at Birkenau, painted a vivid and horrifying picture of life in the camp:

*The sick lie on straw sacks, all jumbled together, one on top of the other, and cannot stretch their sore limbs nor rest their backs. The beds bulge with filth and excrement, and the dead and the decomposing press with their stiffened bodies against the living who, confined as they are, cannot move away. Every illness in the camp is represented here: tuberculosis, diarrhoea, rashes induced by crawling vermin, hunger oedema where the wasted skeleton has filled itself with water to replace the vanished cell tissue, people with bloodshot weals caused by lashes of the whip, people with mangled limbs, frozen feet, wounds from the electric wire, or who have been shot at for trifles by a trigger-happy SS.*

The first major war crimes trials held inside Germany were the two Bergen-Belsen trials conducted by the British in Lüneburg. They predated the Nuremberg trials and were the first to reveal the horrific nature of the camps.

At the first trial, commandant Josef Kramer and 44 SS personnel, functionaries and kapos (trustees) were arraigned. It began on 17 September 1945 and concluded 54 days later, with death sentences being passed on 11 of the defendants. A further 18 were convicted and given prison sentences, 14 were acquitted and one was excused on medical grounds. Within ten years, all those who had been imprisoned were released.

During the trial a Romanian prisoner, Dr Charles Bendel, who had been living in Paris at the time of his internment, had testified to being an eyewitness to the mass extermination of prisoners in August 1944. He had then been assigned to the crematoria as a member of a *Sonderkommando* unit (a work detail forced to dispose of the murdered victims).

Guards from Bergen-Belsen concentration camp are numbered for identification purposes, 1945.

*At about 12 o'clock the new transport arrived with 800 to 1,000 people. They had to undress in the courtyard of the crematorium on a promise of a bath and hot coffee. Their clothing was put on one side and valuables on the other. They entered a big room and there they waited until the gas arrived. The hall was used in winter for the people to undress. Five or ten minutes later the gas arrived in the ambulance, a Red Cross wagon. Then the doors were opened and the people were crowded into the gas chambers. These rooms had such low ceilings that they appeared to come right down on the heads of people. With sticks and blows, these people were forced to go in and stay there, because when they realized they were going to their death, they tried to get out again. Finally they succeeded in locking the doors, hearing cries and shrieks, fighting with each other, and knocking on the wall. This goes on for two minutes and then there is silence; nothing more. Five minutes later the doors were opened, but one could not go near the chambers for twenty minutes after. When the doors were opened a crowd of bodies fell out quite contracted, and it was almost impossible to separate one from the other. They were all compressed together. One got the impression that they had fought terribly against death. Anyone who has seen a gas chamber filled to the height of one and a half metres with corpses will never forget this.*

Dr Bendel testified that at that time the victims had all been transported from the ghetto at Łódź. In all, some 800,000 people were gassed during this operation.

### Vindictive female sadists

Three thousand six hundred German women were employed as guards and SS ancillaries in the concentration camps, but only 60 were indicted for their crimes in the first five years after the war. Minor infractions of the rules were routinely punished by severe beatings with truncheons and whips, which led to the subsequent deaths of many of the weak, overworked and underfed prisoners. Consequently there were few surviving witnesses to testify to the individual acts of wanton cruelty that had led directly to the deaths of inmates. Nevertheless, the trials of these women revealed that they could be as gleefully sadistic and depraved as the very worst of their male colleagues, deriving what one prosecutor described as 'malicious pleasure' from their abuse of power.

The Bergen-Belsen trial put three of these modern harpies in the dock – Irma Grese, Elisabeth Volkenrath and Juana Bormann – who belonged to the *SS-Helferinnenkorps* (Women Helper Corps) or *SS-Gefolge* (Retinue). As such they were not strictly members of the SS, which had been designated as a criminal organization, and therefore they could not be prosecuted for belonging to Himmler's elite but only for the violence they had meted out with their own hands.

Volkenrath was a vindictive sadist who trained her dogs to tear prisoners to pieces. She was just 26 when her murderous reign came to an end. Grese was four years younger when she was found guilty of shooting prisoners indiscriminately and beating others to death. She was also feared for unleashing her dogs on defenceless women inmates, having starved the animals for days to ensure that they would be ravenously hungry when she released them.

Bormann was the eldest. She was 52 when she was indicted for training her wolfhounds to savage prisoners to death.

They were typical of the poorly educated working-class women who applied for jobs in the camps because they offered security of employment, a decent wage and better living conditions than they could have expected in civilian life.

A second Belsen trial was convened in June to try only one defendant – Kazimierz Cegielski, a Polish kapo who was known for his brutal treatment of other prisoners. He was condemned to death and executed on 11 October 1946.

The kapos were despised by their fellow prisoners, who considered them to be no better than collaborators, although some kapos tried to claim that they were only taking the one chance they had to escape the gas chamber. However, many were actively assisting the guards to maintain discipline by beating their fellow prisoners and for that reason they were targeted for attacks as soon as the camps were liberated. At Belsen, 150 of them were hurled out of the windows on to the concrete below, under the eyes of British troops.

## The first Nuremberg trial

*I never dreamed that such cruelty, such bestiality and savagery could really exist in this world ... I made the*

*visit [to Buchenwald] deliberately, in order to be in a position to give first-hand evidence of these things, if ever, in the future, there develops a tendency to charge these allegations merely to 'propaganda'.*
General Eisenhower

The Nuremberg trials, in which 24 leading Nazis were indicted for war crimes, began on 20 November 1945, barely six months after the end of the Second World War. They saw prominent figures from the regime such as Hermann Goering, Albert Speer and Joachim von Ribbentrop summoned before an Allied military tribunal, where they would face the world's press and the general public in open court to answer charges of waging aggressive war, criminal profiteering and crimes against humanity. The latter was a new charge conceived by the Allies to facilitate the prosecution of atrocities committed by the criminal state and its enforcers, the dreaded SS and Gestapo.

But the first trial was not the only one of its kind. Twelve subsequent trials of 'lesser war criminals' were convened in Nuremberg over the course of the following four years, the last one rendering its final verdict on 13 April 1949. Together, these hearings revealed the full horror of Nazi genocide and the blind obedience of Nazi bureaucrats, the so-called 'desk murderers' who organized mass murder as if it was an industrial process.

In the dock many of these arrogant and officious functionaries, who had so recently wielded the power of life and death over tens of thousands of innocent victims, were revealed to be pitiable figures lacking in compassion and conscience, who were now faced with the sordid reality of their actions.

The world was profoundly shocked by the magnitude of their crimes and was barely able to understand how a civilized nation in the 20th century could resort to barbarism on such a scale. Millions had vanished from the face of the earth, buried in anonymous mass graves or reduced to ashes in the ovens of Auschwitz and 15,000 other concentration camps in occupied Europe. An additional 25,000 slave labour camps and similar facilities are believed to have operated under the control of the Nazis or that of their Axis allies, accounting for many millions more. Incredibly, the death toll could have been far higher. During his interrogation, Franz Stangl, commandant of Treblinka, claimed that he could have 'processed' tens of thousands more innocent victims had additional trains been provided.

In the last weeks of the war Hitler had ordered all surviving prisoners to be exterminated and was furious with Himmler when he learned that 20,000 remained alive in Buchenwald. Apparently, Himmler had hoped to use the surviving inmates as a bargaining chip to ensure lenient treatment for himself.

In mid-April 1945, two weeks before he committed suicide, Hitler had told the *Reichsführer SS* to 'make sure that your people don't become sentimental', but there was no chance of that. In many places the SS were in such a hurry to abandon the camps that they hastily improvised. At Gardelegen, for instance, they herded those who could still walk into a barn and set it alight.

Huge numbers of prisoners had been evacuated from the camps as the Allies advanced into Germany and many thousands died at the roadside from hunger, thirst, ill-treatment and exhaustion on these forced marches. Those who survived were too emaciated to eat what they could forage or were offered by the troops who liberated them. At Wolfsburg, a number of the starving slave workers who had been forcibly employed at the Volkswagen factory escaped only to die from eating raw flour.

*The importance of a fair trial*

**For Hitler and his followers there is no punishment on this Earth commensurate with their crimes. But out of love for coming generations we must make an example after the conclusion of the war, so that no one will ever again have the slightest urge to try a similar action.**
Fourth leaflet, anti-Nazi resistance group
The White Rose, July 1942

Although Nazi apologists would later attempt to portray the trials as examples of victors' retribution, the survivors were not seeking revenge, only justice – both for themselves and for those who could not appear to testify on their own behalf. The Allies could not risk allowing the Germans to prosecute their own, as they had done in 1921. That trial of the leaders of the First World War had been seen as an embarrassing failure and a travesty of justice.

This time it was considered necessary to establish beyond all reasonable doubt that Germany's defeated leaders were the architects of its destruction so that the country could renounce its past and begin the process of reconstruction. Churchill and some prominent figures within the American administration expressed the desire to see the captured Nazi leaders executed without trial in order to avoid the 'tangles of legal procedure', while the British foreign secretary Anthony Eden had argued that 'the guilt of such individuals is so black that they fall outside and go beyond the scope of any judicial process'.

The Nazis had denied their victims a fair hearing, so why should they receive a fair trial? There was also the risk that they could use it as a platform to justify their actions and spew forth their vile racist propaganda, as Hitler had done during his trial for treason in Munich in 1923.

But as hungry as Stalin was for revenge, he had warned Churchill that if the regime's leaders were summarily executed the German people might one day recast them as martyrs. The British were acutely aware of what had happened after the leaders of the 1916 Irish rebellion were shot without trial. They became the symbolic figureheads for a revolutionary movement which would dog the British for over 80 years.

Ironically, it was Roosevelt's secretary of war, Henry Stimson, and a colleague from the War Department, Lieutenant Colonel Murray Bernays, who found the solution. The Allies would prosecute the Nazi leaders as former members of a criminal regime which had engaged in a conspiracy to wage aggressive war (i.e. a war that could not be justified as a defence of a country's borders) and enslave the populations of the conquered territories for plunder and profit. It was an approach which would be seen, in Stimson's words, to punish the chief conspirators 'in a dignified manner which will have all the greater effect upon posterity'.

After much argument and delay, the British finally conceded that this would be the best approach and the military tribunal consisting of American, French, Russian and British judges and prosecutors was convened at the former Palace of Justice in Nuremberg. It was one of the few public buildings still standing.

Former US attorney general Robert Jackson was given the onerous task of drafting 'the secular equivalent of the Ten Commandments' to ensure an expeditious trial 'in keeping with our tradition of fairness toward those accused of crime'.

*We will show these men to be the living symbols of racial hatred, terrorism and violence and of the arrogance and cruelty of power.*
Chief Counsel Justice Jackson

*Verdicts*

On 30 September 1946, after a gruelling ten months of hearing often harrowing evidence and routine procedural arguments, the first verdicts were read out. Twelve of the defendants were found guilty and sentenced to hang. They were Luftwaffe chief Hermann Goering, Nazi ambassador Joachim von Ribbentrop, party ideologist Alfred Rosenberg, Field Marshal Wilhelm Keitel, Hans Frank, the former governor-general of Poland, Nazi lawyer and minister of the interior Wilhelm Frick, Jew-baiter and racist publisher Julius Streicher, General Alfred Jodl, Nazi quisling Arthur Seyss-Inquart, *Reichskommissar* in the Netherlands, slave labour czar Fritz Sauckel and Gestapo chief Ernst Kaltenbrunner. Party leader Martin Bormann, Hitler's private secretary and the man considered to be 'the power behind the throne', was sentenced to death *in absentia*.

Keitel's defence that he was only obeying orders was discounted with the comment: 'Superior orders, even to a soldier, cannot be considered in mitigation where crimes as shocking and extensive have been committed consciously, ruthlessly.' Hitler's former deputy Rudolf Hess was found guilty on two counts and sentenced to life imprisonment. His insanity defence was dismissed with the comment: 'There is no suggestion that Hess was not completely sane when the acts charged against him were committed.'

Grand Admiral Karl Doenitz, the Führer's nominal successor, was found guilty on two counts and sentenced to ten years' imprisonment and his subordinate, Admiral Erich Raeder, was found guilty on three counts and sentenced to life imprisonment. Hitler Youth leader Baldur von Schirach received a 20-year sentence, as did Hitler's architect and

Hermann Goering had lost weight rapidly under the enforced diet plan of the Allies, but he cheated the hangman, and those hoping he might admit his guilt, by taking his own life at Nuremberg.

armaments minister Albert Speer. Konstantin von Neurath, Reich protector of Bohemia and Moravia, was given a 15-year sentence but served only eight.

Nazi banker Hjalmar Schacht was acquitted on the grounds that he had been removed from his post before the war began and had spent the last year of the war in Dachau, while Nazi minister Franz von Papen, Hitler's vice-chancellor, was also acquitted. However, Walter Funk, who took over from Schacht as minister of economics, was sentenced to life imprisonment for, among other things, actively promoting the conspirators' access to power. He was released from prison in 1957 and died three years later. Propaganda minister Hans Fritzsche, Goebbels' deputy, was acquitted, but was subsequently sentenced to nine years in prison by a West German denazification court.

Robert Ley, leader of the German Labour Front, had committed suicide in his cell before the trial began, while the 24th defendant, Gustav Krupp, elderly patriarch of the armaments dynasty, was deemed too ill to be tried.

## Executions

At just after one o'clock on the morning of 16 October 1946, von Ribbentrop, the first of the defendants to be convicted and sentenced to death, was taken from his cell to the gymnasium in the courtyard of the prison and led to the scaffold. The other defendants were executed at intervals over the next 90 minutes.

Goering had cheated the hangman only hours before his scheduled execution by biting on a cyanide capsule that had been smuggled into his cell, but his body was also brought into the gymnasium to be photographed along with the others and to be certified dead by the doctor. Just before dawn the bodies were loaded on to trucks and driven under guard to a Munich crematorium. The ashes were scattered in a nearby river. Goebbels' earlier assessment stands as their epitaph:

*At best these are average men. Not one of them has the qualities of a mediocre politician, to say nothing of the calibre of a statesman. They have all remained the beer-cellar rowdies they always were. And in the course of twelve years of easy living many of them have destroyed with drink the little bit of intelligence that once brought them into the movement. This gang of spiteful children, each of whom intrigues against all the rest, whose only thought is of their personal welfare and their standing with the Führer ...*

## The other Nuremberg trials

The Palace of Justice in Nuremberg was the scene of 12 further trials, all of them conducted by the Americans without the participation of their allies. Predictably, these did not attract the worldwide media attention which had accompanied the first trial, but they demonstrated the Americans' determination to pursue the individuals who had implemented Hitler's criminal edicts.

*The Doctors' Trial* began on 9 December 1946 and saw 23 defendants arraigned on charges of conducting unwarranted and sadistic medical 'tests' and 'experiments' on concentration camp inmates and POWs. After hearing testimony from 85 witnesses and examining 1,471 documents over a course of seven months, 16 of the 23 defendants were found guilty. Seven were sentenced to death, nine received substantial prison sentences and seven were acquitted. The executions were carried out in Landsberg Prison, where Hitler had dictated *Mein Kampf* during his imprisonment for leading the failed Munich putsch of 1923.

*The Milch Trial* was held between 2 January and 16 April 1947, when Field Marshal Erhard Milch of the Luftwaffe was arraigned on charges of murder, the inhumane treatment of POWs and participating in unnecessary and unjustifiable medical 'experiments'. Milch was sentenced to life imprisonment, which was subsequently commuted to 15 years. He was released in June 1954, having served only half of his sentence.

*The Judges' Trial* opened on 5 March 1947 and closed on 4 December, with nine members of the Reich Ministry of Justice and seven members of the People's Court answering charges of abusing their powers as prosecutors and members of the judiciary, specifically the imprisonment of alleged 'enemies of the state' and 'judicial murder'. On the opening day, the defendants were arraigned and charged 'with crimes of such immensity that mere specific instances of criminality appear insignificant by comparison ... The dagger of the assassin was concealed beneath the robe of the jurist.'

Ten of the accused were convicted and four acquitted, while another was freed on a technicality and the 16th died in custody. Two of the life sentences were subsequently reduced to 20 years, leaving only one of the accused, Oswald Rothaug, the 'Hanging Judge', in prison after 1951. He was released in 1956.

*The WVHA Trial* summoned 18 officials from the SS Economic and Administrative Office to hear charges relating to the construction and administration of the concentration camps and the exploitation of slave labour. In addition, this branch of the SS organized the wholesale looting of property owned by those who had been transported to the camps, a haul estimated to be in the region of 100 million Reichsmarks. In a statement typical of the Nazi mindset, defendant SS Lieutenant General Oswald Pohl declared: 'In no way am I responsible or guilty for the murder of the five million Jews or the deaths of others in the concentration camps ... The fact that I was in charge of all the concentration camps in Germany from 1942 until the end is beside the point.' Pohl and three of his fellow defendants were found guilty and were sentenced to death, while 11 others received sentences of between ten years and life. Three of the accused were acquitted.

*The Flick Trial*, so called because its chief defendant, Friedrich Flick, had formed a cartel under his own name to confiscate Jewish-owned businesses, saw Flick and five members of his cartel indicted for theft and procuring slave labour. The trial, which dragged on from 19 April until 22 December, found Flick and two of the accused guilty but acquitted three others.

*The Hostage Case* put 12 German generals in the dock on 15 July 1947. They were accused of murdering civilians and captured partisans and POWs during the Balkans campaign and committing various 'acts of devastation' in Norway. Eight were found guilty and sentenced to lengthy prison terms, two were acquitted, one committed suicide before the arraignment and another was excluded on medical grounds. The trial ended on 19 February 1948.

*The IG Farben* trial opened on 27 August 1947 and continued for 11 months, during which the intricacies of the chemical corporation's hierarchy and the extent of its highly profitable cooperation with the dictatorship were outlined in minute detail. Charts and diagrams were pinned on the walls behind the witness stand, illustrating the complex chain of command. This was to enable identification of the men responsible for shaping a corporate policy which facilitated the murder of millions in the gas chambers and allowed the company to profit from the theft of confiscated facilities and property in the conquered territories.

In all, 24 employees were indicted, their main line of defence relying on the spurious argument of 'necessity'. Judge Hebert ruled it inapplicable in this case and damned all the defendants as willing participants in theft, the production and supply of poison gas and the exploitation of slave labour. Nevertheless, the military tribunal decided to acquit ten of the accused and hand down lenient sentences to the remaining defendants.

*The Einsatzgruppen Trial* (29 September 1947–9 April 1948) took its name from the mobile execution units which followed the Wehrmacht into Russia, tasked with the murder of members of the Communist Party and other 'undesirables'. In all there were estimated to be more than a million victims, making this comparatively obscure trial the largest single murder trial in history.

It took the prosecution just two days to present the damning evidence, after which they were obliged to listen to five months of legal wrangling, minor points of procedure and spurious claims from the defence, who attempted to distance their clients from the alleged, but well-documented, atrocities. Perhaps this line of defence was to be expected when eight of the 24 defendants had been members of the legal profession. Incredibly, some of their fellow accused were also highly educated and cultured. One had been an academic, another an opera singer and a third was an art collector.

SS Major General Otto Ohlendorf, commander of *Einsatzgruppe D*, attempted to justify the murder of children on the grounds of 'necessity', claiming that they would have grown into vengeful adults had they been allowed to live. His brazen attempt did not convince the tribunal, who found him guilty of murder and sentenced him to death by hanging, along with 13 of his fellow defendants. Two others received life sentences and five more were convicted and sentenced to prison terms of between ten and 20 years.

*The RuSHA Trial* (29 October 1947–10 March 1948) brought 14 high-ranking officials from the Reich Race and Resettlement Office and its affiliate the Office for the Strengthening of Germanism to account for the deportation, torture and murder of foreign nationals. Only one of the defendants was acquitted, the others receiving various terms of imprisonment.

*The Krupp Trial* ran from 8 December 1947 until 31 July 1948, during which 12 directors and senior employees of the armaments giant, including Alfried, the 38-year-old son of its elderly head, were arraigned on charges relating to the re-armament of Germany and supplying weapons to a criminal regime. Their relationship with Hitler's government was described as 'a veritable alliance' and was compared to an octopus which 'swiftly unfolded its tentacles behind each new aggressive push of the Wehrmacht'. The judges concluded that: 'The wartime activities of the Krupp concern were based in part

Industrialist Alfried Krupp became minister for armament and war production under Hitler and was found guilty after the war of using slave labour in his factories. He served three years in prison.

upon exploitation of other countries and on exploitation and maltreatment of large masses of forced foreign labour.'

Alfried was convicted and sentenced to 12 years in prison, but he was released three years later and was soon back in business. Despite the forfeiture of his property and the dismantling of the factory and other facilities, Krupp Industries was worth £600 million within seven years.

*The High Command Trial* took place on 30 December 1947 and accused 14 high-ranking members of the German High Command and officers of the Wehrmacht, as well as one former admiral, of planning or participating in various atrocities in German-occupied Europe. Two were acquitted and a third committed suicide before the verdict was given, while the rest were convicted and given sentences ranging from three years to life.

*The Ministries Trial* (6 January 1948–13 April 1949) brought 21 members of the Nazi government to hear charges of waging wars of aggression, violating international treaties and crimes against humanity. Nineteen of the accused were found guilty and were sentenced to between four and 25 years in prison.

## The Ravensbrück trials

The British conducted their own series of seven trials in Hamburg of those female guards and male staff who had worked at Ravensbrück, the only concentration camp for women. The judges were all British officers, assisted by a lawyer. Of the 38 defendants, 21 were women.

The first Ravensbrück trial was held from 5 December 1946 to 3 February 1947, at which 16 camp guards and officials were indicted for murder and the maltreatment of inmates. All were found guilty. Eleven were sentenced to death, two were sentenced to 15 years in prison and two to ten years, while one died during the trial. Two of those who had been sentenced to death committed suicide before the sentence could be carried out.

Head nurse Elisabeth Marschall (61) was found guilty of mistreating prisoners and assisting in unnecessary medical experiments, assistant chief warden Dorothea Binz (27) was accused of hacking a prisoner to death with an axe and shooting others, while guard Greta Bösel (39) was charged with participating in the selection process, which involved determining which of the new arrivals would be spared for slave labour and which would be sent straight to the gas chamber.

Three more Ravensbrück staff members escaped from custody before the trial began but all three were subsequently re-arrested. Two were indicted by the French, who were conducting their own trials in Rastatt. They were convicted and executed by firing squad. The third, Friedrich Opitz, was the only defendant at the second Ravensbrück trial, where he was found guilty of kicking a female prisoner to death and of encouraging his subordinates to do the same. He was sentenced to death.

The third Ravensbrück trial in April 1948 witnessed the indictment of five female guards accused of murder and the ill-treatment of young girls at the Uckermark satellite camp. Two were acquitted because they had been employed when the camp still held only German juveniles, whose fate did not come under the jurisdiction of the British military authorities, one received a life sentence and another ten years' imprisonment, leaving *SS Oberaufseherin* Ruth Closius (Neudeck) to face the hangman alone. She had been found guilty of torturing and murdering men, women and children and of slitting a prisoner's throat with a shovel.

The fourth Ravensbrück trial began in May 1948, with five members of the medical staff in the dock to answer charges of mistreatment and torture. Both of the doctors and one nurse were sentenced to death and two nurses were given sentences

Mugshot of Hans Pflaum, so-called labour director at Ravensbrück, who was executed by firing squad in 1950.

of four and ten years in prison. The death sentence imposed on nurse Gerda Ganzer was subsequently commuted to life imprisonment and was later further reduced to 12 years.

That same month, at the fifth Ravensbrück trial, three SS men were convicted of having murdered Allied inmates. One of the accused was sentenced to death, another to a nominal two years in prison and the third to 20 years, although he was released after spending only six years in jail.

The following month, in the sixth Ravensbrück trial, two SS wardens received prison sentences of ten and 15 years apiece for the mistreatment of Allied prisoners.

The seventh and final trial in July 1948 saw six female wardens in the dock. Two of them were executed, two were sentenced to three and 12 years respectively and two were acquitted for lack of evidence.

## The Dachau trials

*Not to try these beasts would miss the educational and therapeutic opportunity of our generation.*
US Lieutenant Colonel Murray Bernays

The Dachau trials were conducted by an American military tribunal over a three-year period from 1945 to 1947, on the site of the former concentration camp outside Munich. During the first four trials, 177 former administrators and guards stood trial on charges related to atrocities committed at Dachau, Mauthausen, Buchenwald and Flossenbürg and all were convicted. In total 97 defendants were condemned to death, although a third of these sentences were subsequently commuted to life imprisonment, with 54 defendants being given life sentences. The remainder received lengthy terms of imprisonment. In addition, 27 officials, SS guards and kapos were convicted in the Mühldorf and Dora-Nordhausen trials that also took place at Dachau.

The camp was also the location for the prosecution of 73 *Waffen SS* men accused of participating in the Malmedy massacre of 84 American POWs during the Battle of the Bulge in December 1944 and the indictment of German civilians who had murdered captured Allied pilots.

The Dachau trials established the precedent of 'common design' or collective guilt, which assumed that the accused had consented to participate in a joint plan to commit atrocities. It was not necessary for the prosecution to prove that each of the defendants had committed a crime, as by virtue of their employment in the camp they were deemed to be participating in a criminal enterprise. Merely working in a camp where prisoners were maltreated, tortured, exploited and executed was considered to be in violation of the Laws and Usages of War as defined by the Geneva Convention of 1929 and the Hague Convention of 1907, thereby refuting the accusation made by Nazi apologists that these trials were conducted using retrogressive laws to serve the victors and punish their former enemy.

An estimated 30,000 German war criminals were held at Dachau (renamed War Crimes Enclosure No. 1) for up to two years before being released, because the Allies did not have the resources to prosecute them. The first trial, the Dachau Camp trial, saw 40 officials convicted in the winter of 1945, all of whom were found guilty. Thirty-six were sentenced to death, including the commandant, Martin Weiss.

*The Mauthausen trial* indicted 61 officials in the spring of 1946. All but three were sentenced to death including SS doctor Friedrich Entress, who had conducted sadistic experiments on hundreds of prisoners. Nine of these sentences were later commuted to life imprisonment. A second Mauthausen trial was convened in August 1947 and ended with one of the camp's administrators being acquitted, one receiving a life sentence, two being sent to prison for nominal terms and four sentenced to death.

*The Flossenbürg Camp trial* (12 June 1946–19 January 1947) brought 52 officials and guards to trial, of whom 15 were sentenced to death, 11 were given life sentences and 14 were sentenced to short terms of imprisonment. The camp had been the final destination for many of the regime's most vociferous enemies, including the theologian Dietrich Bonhoeffer, Admiral Canaris and various members of the German resistance, as well as many captured SOE agents, who were executed at the camp in the final days of the war.

*The Buchenwald Camp trial* was held between April and August 1947 and saw 31 defendants convicted, of whom 22 received death sentences, including Ilse Koch, wife of the first commandant. More guards would have appeared in the dock had not 80 of them been killed by former inmates, who were said to have been given a free hand by their American liberators.

Its satellite camp at Ohrdruf, near Gotha, contained 10,000 slave workers, several hundred of whom were shot in the final days by SS extermination squads. There were also mounds of emaciated bodies so thin and stiff that they were thought at first to be planks of wood.

Historian Robert H. Abzug, author of *Inside the Vicious Heart: Americans and the Liberation of Nazi Concentration Camps*, describes the survivors as having been reduced to scavenging animals, snatching at the food they were given and scurrying into corners to defend it from their fellow prisoners.

When Generals Eisenhower, Patton and Bradley toured the camp on 12 April, Patton was physically sick from the sight and the overpowering smell. It was on this occasion that he famously remarked to an aide who had advocated leniency towards the Germans: 'Still have trouble hating them?'

Eisenhower issued an order that all units which were not in the front line should visit the camp and see for themselves what National Socialism had led to. 'We are told the US soldier doesn't know what he is fighting for,' he remarked. 'Now, at least, he will know what he is fighting against.'

Ohrdruf was one of many small towns throughout Germany where prisoners had been working under armed guard on building projects, giving the lie to the claim that the population had no idea that the inmates of the camps were abused and ill-treated.

*The Mühldorf Camp trial* in May 1947 ended with five officials sentenced to death and seven imprisoned. Mühldorf was a complex of camps near Mettenheim in Bavaria, whose function was to provide slave labour for the construction of the underground factories which would produce the Me-262 jet fighter and other 'war-winning' secret weapons. Inmates were worked up to 12 hours a day and being considered expendable they were used to excavate caves and dig tunnels through the mountains at considerable personal risk.

*The Dora-Nordhausen trial* in August 1947 was the final trial held at Dachau, when 15 former SS guards and kapos were convicted of war crimes. This camp in Thuringia was where forced labourers were detained while working on the V2 rocket. Twelve thousand slave workers were housed in tunnels where up to 75 died every day from starvation, maltreatment and disease. There were 3,000 unburied bodies when the Americans liberated the camp and 700 other prisoners were on the verge of death. The town's citizens were forcibly marched to the site and ordered to bury the dead.

The German state's own war crimes trials continued infrequently into the 1960s, with the Belzec trial of eight SS men in Munich, the Chełmno trials in Bonn, the Auschwitz trials in Frankfurt, the Sobibór trial in Hagen and the first Treblinka trial in Düsseldorf. However, the second Treblinka trial did not end until December 1970 and the Majdanek trials did not conclude until the early 1980s. These later trials were historically significant because they marked the first time that Nazi crimes against German nationals were heard. In previous war crimes trials the Allies had only prosecuted crimes against Allied citizens and prisoners of war.

## The significance of the trials

The trials stimulated heated debate around the world and raised numerous issues, one of which was whether the victors had a right to judge their defeated enemy. Another question was whether the victors could condemn the behaviour of their enemy when they themselves were not entirely innocent or blameless, having made use of indiscriminate bombing to achieve that victory. Addressing the latter concern shortly after the last trial was concluded, the chief prosecutor, Brigadier General Telford Taylor, told the International News Service:

*... these anxieties spring from the notion that at Nuremberg the Nazi diplomats were punished for drafting notes, the generals for making military plans and the businessmen for manufacturing war materials – things that were done by our own diplomats and generals and businessmen ... No Nuremberg defendant was accused or convicted merely because he held a high position, or performed a particular function, but only upon a showing that he used or abused the position, authority or skill in a criminal manner.*

Nuremberg established the need and precedent for such calculated and cold-blooded crimes to be tried by internationally constituted courts and, in doing so, it not only guaranteed that those who commit such crimes in the future will be held accountable for their actions, but that their surviving victims will also have the right to bear witness in a public court.

After the final verdicts had been read out, no head of state could claim that they were above the law or had the right to violate international treaties in their treatment of prisoners, nor could they say that they were unaware of what constituted a war crime. Furthermore, no government functionary or member of the armed forces could evade their personal responsibilities or seek to excuse their complicity in a war crime by claiming that they were merely obeying orders, acting under duress or serving the state.

Nuremberg not only established the basis of international law on human rights, but it also formulated the law governing the conduct of war. The fact that flagrant abuses of human rights continue to be perpetrated on defenceless victims by both democratic and totalitarian governments does not betray a flaw in the precedents established at Nuremberg. It is a failing of those who are unwilling or unable to enforce them.

On a more emotional level, it could be argued that the Nuremberg trials and those hearings held elsewhere in the immediate post-war years served to offer some form of closure or catharsis for both the Allies and their former enemy. It is true, and extremely galling, that so many of the guilty escaped justice and that countless others returned to their former lives convinced that they had done nothing to be ashamed of, but in an imperfect world there can be no true accounting. Nuremberg, however, gave some measure of justice in as fair and impartial a manner as was possible in that place, at that time and under those circumstances.

*The criminals and their wretched deeds may pass from memory, but the trials we have no right to forget ... The great question today is not whether the Nuremberg principles are valid, but whether mankind can live up to them, and whether it can live at all if it fails.*

Brigadier General Telford Taylor,
Final Report to the Army, 1949

## Chapter Three

# DENAZIFICATION

## Facing the consequences

If it is true that the majority of Germans lived in denial of their nation's past, then the day they were forced to face the unpalatable facts of Nazi tyranny must be seen as the first significant stage in denazification.

The Americans who liberated Buchenwald concentration camp on 11 April 1945 were shocked, disgusted and incensed by what they saw. They couldn't take their anger out on the civilians, whom they suspected of being passively complicit in the crimes by supporting the regime, so they settled for compelling them to tour the camp, which was still littered with mounds of emaciated cadavers and reeked of death and decay.

Four days after the liberation of Buchenwald, one of the largest camps operating inside Germany, up to 1,000 local residents were escorted through the gas chambers, the crematoria and the overcrowded infirmary by armed US soldiers. Many were seen smiling for the newsreel camera as they approached, obviously expecting to see something that had been staged for their benefit, but they were not smiling when they left. They saw for themselves the piles of human bones, the gallows and some of the skeletal survivors still clothed in tattered, filthy rags. There was also a small display of gruesome exhibits including human organs preserved in glass jars, shrunken heads and strips of tattooed skin inscribed with what the newsreel described as 'indecent' drawings.

Some doubtless dismissed the images from their minds as soon as they returned to their homes, but for many the sight and the smell lingered with them for the rest of their lives. Many of the women who witnessed the consequences of Nazi persecution and racial policy that day were moved to tears, while a few found it too much and fainted.

Inmate Imre Kertész, a Hungarian writer, was 15 years old the day the citizens of Weimar came to stare at the chamber of horrors. He recalled them being dressed in their best Sunday clothes. The women had done their hair and put on their more fashionable hats after being told that they were to be filmed touring a Nazi facility outside the town. On being shown a mass grave, some of the men removed their hats while others covered their faces, but all fell silent. Then they looked at the Americans, raised their arms in mute disbelief and shook their heads. 'They knew nothing about it,' said Kertész. 'No one knew anything about it.'

It was not uncommon for the mounds of rotting flesh to be dismissed as the victims of Allied bombing raids, a lie that had originated with Nazi spin doctor Dr Joseph Goebbels.

That same week the celebrated American journalist Edward R. Murrow broadcast a report from Buchenwald to a radio audience of millions back in the United States. For many, liberation had come too late. They were beyond saving, despite the efforts of the Red Cross and US medical staff. In the camp hospital Murrow was told that 200 patients had died in a single day from starvation, fatigue and tuberculosis. Some were simply worn out and lacked the will to live. Their daily ration was now just one piece of brown bread as thick as a thumb covered with margarine and maybe a small portion of stew. Any more and their weakened constitutions wouldn't be able to digest it. Too much food was fatal to a starving person. Just half a mile away on the other side of the barbed wire he observed well-fed German farmers tending their fields.

Similar scenes were recorded by Allied cameramen at Dachau outside Munich and many other camps. There the piles of abandoned clothes, shoes and spectacles testified to the most recent victims of Nazi genocide, who had been ordered to undress in preparation for taking a shower. In some cases they had even been provided with soap and towels before being herded into gas chambers complete with dummy shower heads. Their bodies were waiting to be cremated in the ovens of the crematoria.

In a forest outside the medieval city of Nuremberg, the picturesque setting for the Nazis' annual party rallies, the Allies unearthed evidence of a massacre of Polish Jews. Instead of merely compelling the local population to view the bodies, they ordered them to bury the victims. But first they were forced to carry the wooden coffins through the streets where only a few years earlier the SA and the SS had paraded on their way to the Zeppelin Field, where Hitler would address a crowd of up to 200,000 loyal followers. On this occasion there were no strutting stormtroopers in their brown shirts and jackboots and no military bands and banners. Instead, there were just sullen, silent faces and maybe one or more of them asking themselves how it had come to this.

# Re-education of Germans

*I have yet to find a German who*
*will admit to being a Nazi.*
Margaret Bourke-White, American photojournalist

After Germany's defeat in 1918 the Allies were satisfied that they had won a decisive victory over German imperialism. They deemed it sufficient to impose punitive reparations, occupy the demilitarized Rhineland and demand the abdication of the Kaiser in order symbolically to behead a belligerent aggressor.

But in 1945 they knew that it was not enough to decapitate the dictatorship and occupy the country and they realized that levying reparations might feed resentment that could lead to a third and possibly apocalyptic world war. The enemy of 1939–45 was more than a military adversary; it was an ideology. Disarming the enemy's armed forces, imprisoning its combatants and imposing martial law would not address the root cause of the conflict that had cost the victors more than any military campaign in history.

Forcing the general population to face the horrifying consequences of their enthusiastic support for the Hitler regime by making them tour the concentration, extermination and forced labour camps was distressing for some – in one town the mayor and his wife hanged themselves afterwards – but it was not enough. Accepting complicity in a crime in which you did not actively participate takes extraordinary courage, which few possess or are even willing to consider. It was not enough, either, to put the surviving Nazi leaders on trial in a public courtroom and prosecute them for war crimes and crimes against humanity, a charge conceived by the Allies specifically to address Nazi atrocities. Revealing the true nature of the dictatorship and having the accused admit their guilt under cross-examination would still not be enough to convince diehard believers that National Socialism was an iniquitous and malignant threat to civilization.

The Germans had been indoctrinated with a pernicious ideology and were conditioned to believe that they were superior beings, the Aryan Master Race, destined to rule over the *Untermenschen* – the subhumans and 'inferior' races. Until their distorted perception could be contested and their perverse 'philosophy' had been proven a fallacy, they would continue to see themselves as victims and the Allies as the aggressor. It was common for the occupying armies to be berated by angry, resentful citizens and be accused of having brought misery and deprivation unnecessarily upon 'innocent' Germans. As one woman expressed it: 'None of this would have happened if you had surrendered in 1940.'

A survey conducted by the American Military Government in the American zone in 1948 revealed that only 30 per cent of those polled believed that National Socialism was a 'bad idea' and that twice as many believed that Nazism was a 'good idea badly carried out'.

The same number declared their preference for a government which offered economic security and the possibility of a decent income over one which guaranteed free elections, freedom of speech, a free press and religious freedom. Evidently, the Nazi mentality had outlived the regime.

Playwright Bertolt Brecht was angered by what he called the Germans' 'good-natured cluelessness, the shamelessness, that they were simply continuing on as if it were only their houses that had been destroyed'. The only solution was to re-educate the people in order to rid them of their delusions and erroneous beliefs, which was a problematic and potentially impossible task.

## Many Germans were still Nazis

*The Germans act as if the Nazis were a strange race [...] who invaded Germany.*
Unnamed American major quoted by
Margaret Bourke-White in *Dear Fatherland*, 1946

In May 1945 approximately one in ten of the population were paid-up members of the Nazi Party. Eight million were still staunch supporters of the regime and as many as 37 million more shared Hitler's beliefs, if membership of the affiliated organizations was an accurate indication of their convictions. For all the bland assurances and protests of innocence which greeted the Allies ('Tommy, me no Nazi' was a standard greeting), the fact was that Hitler's racist doctrines had been endorsed by a significant section of the population and they would not renounce their ingrained beliefs and convictions overnight.

As the anti-Nazi resistance group The White Rose had pointed out in June 1942:

*It is impossible to engage in intellectual discourse with National Socialist Philosophy, for if there were*

*such an entity, one would have to try by means of
analysis and discussion either to prove its validity or
to combat it. In actuality, however, we face a totally
different situation. At its very inception this movement
depended on the deception and betrayal of one's
fellow man; even at that time it was inwardly corrupt
and could support itself only by constant lies.*

A proportion may have subscribed to the Nazi creed purely for
self-preservation, as party membership was required in order
to work in certain areas of public life. Others may have joined
in the hope of advancement, or to be seen to conform, and
in doing so ensure that their loyalty to the regime was never
questioned. However, the vast majority had enrolled because
they sincerely believed in National Socialism and had gambled
on their anonymity to see them through the filtering process
that became known as denazification. It was an impractical and
impossible task, but it had to be seen to be done in order to
ensure that Nazi officials were not allowed to return to positions
of power – no matter how lowly – and to demonstrate to the
free world that a criminal state was being purged of its most
malignant elements.

The European Advisory Commission, which, among other
tasks, had been entrusted with the practicalities of Germany's
surrender, had provided the occupation forces with a list of
Nazi organizations and state functionaries who were subject to
automatic arrest. Among the first to be rounded up and interned
were officials of the German Labour Front, the German Red
Cross (who had facilitated the euthanasia programme) and

the Gestapo. These were joined by key industrialists who had financed Hitler's war machine and high-profile artists and other public figures whose faces had appeared in Nazi newsreels, peddling their propaganda. Lesser figures were identified and located thanks to their surviving victims and those political opponents of the regime who had managed to evade arrest, imprisonment and execution. But with so many refugees on the move, it was easy for minor party officials, former concentration camp guards and other functionaries to lose themselves in the anonymous multitudes migrating from east to west and 'misplace' their identification papers en route.

It was not so easy, though, for SS members, who had their blood group tattooed on their arms; consequently, numerous members of Himmler's elite were soon identified and executed. Some who had been former guards in the camps tried to evade arrest by donning the striped uniforms worn by the inmates, but they were quickly identified by their well-fed appearance and beaten by brutalized prisoners.

At Dachau, near Munich, the first American officer on the scene struggled to maintain discipline after his men found 2,310 emaciated bodies, including those of 21 children, on the last train to arrive at the concentration camp. They had died from malnutrition, dehydration and suffocation after being crammed into the cattle wagons. At first the officer thought he was looking at a mound of rags rather than human beings. On arrival at Dachau they had been set upon by dogs, shot or beaten to death by rifle butts wielded by the SS. Many of the young American soldiers broke down and wept, while others were all for shooting the captured SS guards on the spot, one of whom had machine-gunned prisoners who had left the relative safety of their huts to greet their liberators. After witnessing that massacre, one GI could not be restrained and let loose with his own machine gun. He is thought to have killed as many as 122 SS prisoners before an officer physically restrained him.

Some of the inmates were content to humiliate their former tormentors by ordering them to doff their caps in salute, while others sought retribution by attacking the guards with whatever came to hand. A few presumed upon the Americans to lend them a bayonet or other weapon and the GIs were often too shaken up to refuse. In all, about 40 SS and kapos were butchered by prisoners on that day in Dachau.

In the East it was the Prussian nobility, the Junkers, and the landowners who faced retribution at the hands of the Soviet forces. Although some protested (with justification) that they were anti-Nazi, they were seen as the enemy by the Communists and were killed or hauled off to Russian gulags, where they endured privations and brutality equal to that experienced by inmates in the Nazi labour camps.

## Nazi industrialists evade justice

In the West, some of the biggest industrialists escaped justice. Alfried Krupp, the 37-year-old head of the German armaments manufacturer, was released after a cursory interview and returned to his vast estate on the outskirts of Essen. He was then placed under house arrest and waited on by a staff of 100 while the Allies pondered what to do with him. His 75-year-old father, Gustav, the nominal head of the dynasty, was apparently too ill to stand trial, so Alfried was considered a prime candidate to sit alongside Goering, Ribbentrop, Keitel and the other big names in the dock at Nuremberg. In the end, there was deemed to be insufficient time to prepare a case against him and he was let off the hook. He was subsequently indicted at a later trial and sentenced to 12 years in prison, of which he served only three.

Walter Rohland, or 'Panzer Rohland' as he was known on account of his contribution to German steel production, was persuaded to serve as a prosecution witness against Krupp and was subsequently allowed to remain at liberty in spite of his enormous contribution to German tank production.

Even more controversial and emotive was the failure to bring the directors of IG Farben to account. The chemical company had produced poison gas, nerve gas, weapons and explosives for the German Army, but it was the production and supply of Zyklon B, a derivative of an industrial pesticide, that saw 24 of its former employees indicted at Nuremberg in August 1947. It had been used to exterminate hundreds of thousands of victims in the gas chambers of Nazi concentration camps. They were charged with other crimes too, namely the exploitation of slave labour and the theft of private property in the German-occupied territories, but ten of the defendants were still set free and the remainder received comparatively lenient sentences. Heinrich Bütefisch, the firm's head of production at Auschwitz, received only six years in prison and board member Dr Georg von Schnitzler, a former member of the SA, got off even more lightly, although he had been instrumental in the acquisition of slave labour and had admitted that his company had given 'substantial and even decisive aid' to the regime and 'was largely responsible for the policies of Hitler'. Despite being named one of Nazi Germany's prominent war economy leaders he was sentenced to a nominal five years in prison, of which he served just 12 months.

In the British zone there was a marked discrepancy between senior army officers, who were eager to bring to justice those accused of war crimes, and the judiciary, who were acutely aware that they needed to be seen to be conducting a fair trial. This disparity was highlighted by comments made during the trial of Josef Kramer, commandant of Auschwitz and later Bergen-Belsen, by the British Army's Judge Advocate General Carl Ludwig Stirling, a civilian barrister with a reputation as a stickler for procedure. Stirling angered many on the British side by warning the military tribunal that the court could not convict solely on the basis that the defendants had been members of the staff employed at Belsen or Auschwitz. They needed, he said, to be convinced that the accused was personally guilty of war crimes and not merely guilty by association.

The British prime minister, Clement Atlee, felt the need to express his disapproval by writing to Stirling's superior, the secretary of state for war, aware that such comments had received widespread publicity and may have influenced many former Nazis to take their chances in the British rather than the American zone. Fourteen of Kramer's fellow defendants in the Belsen trial were acquitted, in stark contrast to the Dachau trial conducted by the Americans, which ended with guilty verdicts being passed on all 40 of the accused, 36 of whom were sentenced to death. The Belsen trial would be the last major war crimes trial conducted in the British zone. Thereafter each nation would be responsible for prosecuting those who had murdered its own citizens.

The inconsistency in the attitude of the two former allies towards the prosecution of war criminals was further underlined by the fact that the British did not make completion of the denazification questionnaire compulsory for every German adult in their zone, but only for those employed in the public sector or applying for jobs in public organizations and businesses.

Former Nazis simply had to content themselves with being employed in lowly positions to avoid detection until the British handed over the responsibility for denazification to the newly elected German regional administrations in October 1947.

The French were more consistent in their approach to weeding out ardent Nazis, although they only managed to identify 13 major offenders and classify a paltry 18,000 as belonging to the lesser categories. This was partly due to the size of their comparatively small zone, but also to the fact that they only issued questionnaires to one in seven Germans living under their authority.

## The Nazi files

But if the millions of former party members imagined that their anonymity would be preserved in the chaos and disorder, they were soon disillusioned.

On 15 April 1945 the first of 180 trucks drove into the yard of the Josef Wirth paper mill in a suburb of Munich, with bales of paper to be recycled. The manager of the mill, Hans Huber, had been told to expect the deliveries from NSDAP headquarters and to ensure that pulping of the bales received top priority. Huber, an anti-Nazi, was naturally suspicious and although paper was then in short supply he was reluctant to pulp so much without examining it. To his astonishment, he discovered that the bales contained the index cards of every member of the party since its formation, all eight million of them. On each card was a name and address, a career summary and, most usefully, a photograph. According to author Tom Bower in *The Pledge Betrayed*, the total haul amounted to more than 50 tons.

But how could Huber avoid destroying the bales for long enough to be able to hand them over to the Allies? He later claimed that he simply had them stored in a corner of the mill and when the party officials returned to check that their instructions were being carried out, he told them that those were bales belonging to other customers, whose work had to be postponed while he was processing the party's priority order.

On 30 April, Munich, the crucible of National Socialism, was captured by the Americans and the files were eventually transported to the Ministerial Collecting Centre near Kassel. There they were examined by former German government officials, who were assisting the Americans in collating and sifting through mountains of documents in order to identify former Nazi officials and war criminals.

## What kind of Nazi were you?

According to Perry Biddiscombe, author of *The Denazification of Germany*, the process of identifying and eliminating from public life all of the former Nazis in post-war Germany was rendered impractical because of the sheer number involved. In addition to the eight million party members, there were an additional ten million members from each of the affiliated organizations, including the Hitler Youth. The total was believed to be some 45 million and if each and every one of these individuals were to be imprisoned or excluded from contributing to the regeneration of the country, only half of the population would be working; not enough to get the economy up and running again.

The urgency of the situation was highlighted by the Peine mining disaster near Hanover in December 1945, in which 46 men died and many more were seriously injured. The accident was attributed to human error and it was felt that it could have been prevented had there been enough senior engineers to supervise safety procedures. However, they had been dismissed because of their former membership of the Nazi Party. Six weeks later, on 20 February 1946, a second and more costly disaster occurred at Unna near Dortmund, which claimed the lives of 417 men. It was the worst coal mining disaster in German history and again the fatalities were blamed in a large part on the absence of senior mining officials. The director of the mine had been jailed for belonging to the party and a senior inspector had only recently been released but had returned to work in a state of mental collapse. More lives might have been lost had the director not been released to organize the rescue of 57 men who had been trapped underground by an explosion.

Both tragedies had occurred in the British zone and consequently the British administration was held responsible by the local inhabitants, who viewed the expulsion of party members as short-sighted and imprudent. In a characteristic piece of English understatement, Arthur Street, a senior civil servant in the British occupation zone reported: 'We are very much alive to the dangers inherent of too drastic a policy of denazification in industry.' As a consequence of this reappraisal over 300 German mining officials were released from custody in the British zone and reinstated, leaving only 20 in jail.

It was decided that the most sensible approach to the problem was to issue a 12-page questionnaire (*Fragebogen*) to every German citizen, to help identify those who were active party members and those who had joined in the wake of the 1933 Reichstag elections (the so-called *Märzgefallenen* and *Maiveilchen*), and so could be assumed to have joined as a matter of expediency. The final five classifications were 'Exonerated', 'Followers' (aka Fellow Travellers), 'Less Incriminated', 'Incriminated' (Activists, Militants and Profiteers) and 'Major Offenders'.

Between 1946 and 1948, 16 million questionnaires were distributed in the three western zones. Among the 133 questions were a number relating to physical description, political affiliations, financial details and family ancestry.

The latter question was intended to identify members of the Junkers nobility, in the belief that they had enabled Hitler to rise to power. Other questions required the respondent to give full details of their military service and to admit if they had profited or benefitted in any way from the theft of Jewish property under the regime's Aryanization policy.

Additional pages were provided for personal comments, which offered individuals the opportunity to explain why they had joined Nazi organizations or voted for the Nazi Party, but also left space for them to denounce fellow citizens, who may have been unpaid Gestapo informers and were therefore unknown to the Allies.

It was the largest sociological survey of its kind and though it was flawed in many ways – not the least of which was its reliance on the honesty of the respondent and the fact that non-compliance with Nazi policy had not been an option – it offers historians a valuable insight into the way ordinary Germans saw themselves and their relationship to the regime. For many this meant constructing a false identity as a helpless victim.

Austria's citizens had welcomed Hitler back to his *Heimat* after the *Anschluss* in March 1938, but they now recast themselves as

Window shoppers gaze longingly at pastries temptingly laid out before their eyes by a Viennese bakery, but few could afford such luxuries in the post-war economy.

'the first victims' of Nazi aggression. The Austrian authorities were accused of being too lenient with former Nazis and suspiciously negligent in accumulating evidence against alleged mass murderers. Special People's Courts had passed only seven death sentences on Nazi war criminals by the end of 1945, in a country where there were deemed to be as many as 50,000 top category Nazis – those officially classified as 'incriminated' (i.e. implicated) in war crimes. Only half of that number were officially investigated and just 13,000 convicted and yet one in ten of the population had been paid-up party members and more than a million Austrians had served in the German military during the war. Now these same men were sporting traditional Tyrolean hats which they would have considered *kitschig* ('corny') before the war, as if recasting themselves as conservative, middle-class Viennese.

Of the more than 60,000 Austrian public officials dismissed from their posts after the war, over half were reinstated within two years.

## End of denazification

The Allies also made exceptions as a matter of expediency. For example, 765 German rocket scientists and engineers, who only months before had been developing Hitler's devastating secret weapons, were spirited away in the night to work for NASA without having to submit to the denazification process. The Russians did the same. In many cases the men's families were also granted visas in order to mollify those who were to contribute to the space race. National security evidently took priority over all other considerations.

Both the Russians and the Americans, and to a lesser extent the British and the French, made these former Nazis an offer they couldn't refuse – decent salaries and top-notch facilities and living conditions. Alternatively, they could stay and face the consequences of having served a criminal state.

Inevitably, the will to prosecute and the ability to prosecute became irreconcilable. There simply wasn't the machinery nor the time to sift through the personal files of the 72,000 Germans interned in the British and American zones, nor the additional 45,000 party officials still at liberty and the 200,000 Gestapo and SS agents who would have had a case to answer. On 4 March 1946, the Denazification Committee estimated that they had the resources to prosecute a tenth of the cases at best.

The likelihood that even a fraction of the cases that were in preparation would be heard was further weakened by the fact that there were simply not enough German lawyers to defend such a huge number of clients. Ninety per cent of the legal profession in post-war Germany had belonged to the Nazi-approved Lawyers' Organization.

And all the time pressure was on the Allied governments to demobilize conscripted men and return to peacetime conditions as soon as practically possible. By the summer of 1946, the Americans had only 200,000 men in Germany to police the peace and enforce the decisions made by the American administrators of the questionnaire – which had been completed in German, a language few of the American troops or their officers could understand.

After sifting through more than a million and a half *Fragebogen*, 374,000 former Nazi Party members were either discharged or reassigned to menial and mundane jobs, leaving 115,000 in prison camps awaiting further processing. Twenty-five thousand of these were categorized as major offenders requiring further investigation. As Frederick Taylor notes in *Exorcising Hitler*, this left three and a half million former Nazis, who were considered to be 'hostile to Allied purposes', excluded from contributing to the economy and to society, among them teachers, doctors, farmers and members of other essential occupations. In Stuttgart, there were 80,000 cases arising from the *Fragebogen* awaiting appraisal, which would have taken years to process.

Faced with the prospect of failure, US General Clay, Military Governor of the US Zone of Occupation, passed the buck back to the Germans. In November 1945, he empowered a commission of known anti-Nazis to put their own house in order. The Denazification Policy Board was chaired by Wilhelm Hoegner, the Bavarian premier, a former Social Democrat who had spent the war in neutral Switzerland. By the following spring, Hoegner and his colleagues had drafted 'the Liberation Law', as it was commonly known, in consultation with the Office of the Military Governor in the American zone.

The 'Law for Liberation from National Socialism and Militarism' set out to 'secure a lasting base for German democratic national life' and to exclude former supporters of National Socialist 'tyranny' from 'public, economic and cultural life'. Those individuals who were guilty of having 'violated the principles of justice and humanity' would be 'called to account' and given the opportunity to answer the charges.

The denazification tribunals which were set up as a result of the 'Liberation Law' were not infallible and were frequently far too lenient, while their individual members were often vulnerable to intimidation or corruption, but it was the first significant step to purging the German psyche of Nazi dogma and exorcizing the long shadow of Hitler.

Weeding the ex-Nazis out was not the problem but keeping them out was. Between 1945 and 1947, one third of former Nazi Party members employed in the American zone were discharged from their jobs only to be re-employed by the end of 1947.

The following year, 85 per cent of civil servants in Hesse were found to be former Nazi Party members who had been dismissed from their posts just a few years earlier, and by August 1950 a quarter of government departments in Bonn were controlled by ex-Nazis who had wormed their way back into the ministries.

In the GDR the proportion was far smaller, but it seemed that the Soviets, too, could turn a blind eye if it served their purpose. Fifteen per cent of the Socialist Unity Party had been card-carrying members of the NSDAP.

The outbreak of the Korean War in June 1950, which threatened to increase communist influence in East Asia, was a decisive factor in distracting the Americans from completing the denazification process and pursuing their former enemies. But denazification could not go on indefinitely because at some point the need to build the future outweighed the need to expunge the past.

In May 1951 the new democratic government of West Germany passed the Law to End Denazification and in doing so closed the darkest chapter in German history.

## Named and shamed

In December 2011 the main opposition party in Germany forced Chancellor Angela Merkel's administration to commission a parliamentary inquiry to investigate the political affiliations of former members of the West German government. It revealed the fact that one former premier, a chancellor and 25 cabinet ministers all had something to hide, namely that they had actively implemented Nazi policy during the Hitler years. Moreover, after the war these former Nazis had sought to cover their tracks by aligning themselves with parties which were not necessarily right-wing, nationalist or even conservative.

The 85-page report became a bestseller and the furore prompted further searches into the archives held by other ministries, the police and also the West German intelligence agencies. The disclosures raised uncomfortable questions regarding the degree to which former Nazis might have influenced the post-war democratic government and its foreign policy, particularly in the Middle East. It was alleged that some diplomats had protected Nazi war criminals then hiding in Africa and South America. All this against accusations that there was substantial 'covering up, denying and suppressing' not only by civil servants but also by influential members of the German media, who wished to conceal the extent of their involvement with the dictatorship. An estimated 800 former Nazis were said to have been given coded warnings by the German Foreign Office not to travel to France, where they had been tried and convicted in their absence and would have risked arrest and prosecution for their wartime activities.

Konrad Adenauer, post-war Germany's first chancellor and an ardent anti-Nazi, called for 'an end to this sniffing out of Nazis' because he believed the new democratic administration needed experienced ministers regardless of their previous misdeeds. For that reason he appointed Hans Globke as his senior state secretary. Globke was the lawyer who had helped draft the infamous Nuremberg Laws, which denied German and Austrian Jews their civil rights. He was so adept at playing both sides that he had the dubious distinction of appearing for both the prosecution and the defence at Nuremberg.

The report also disclosed that the German domestic intelligence service (Bfv) knowingly hired former SS and SD men who had worked for the Gestapo as surveillance experts. However, they were employed as freelancers to keep them at a respectable distance, because they were considered 'tainted'.

The Federal Office of Criminal Investigation (BKA) was known to have former members of the SS Panzer Division *Totenkopf* ('Death's Head', initially made up of concentration camp guards) in key roles – two-thirds of the senior positions according to one estimate. In

1960, it was believed that a quarter of the BKA staff were suspected of being former Nazis and therefore not people to be entrusted with prosecuting their former associates.

## Ex-Nazi lawyers and judges

According to an official internal government report published in 2015, more than half of the 170 lawyers and judges employed in the West German Justice Ministry between 1949 and 1973 were found to have been former members of the Nazi Party. Thirty-four of them had belonged to the *Sturmabteilung* (SA), the Brown Shirt paramilitary thugs who had served as Hitler's bodyguard and Nazi Party enforcers. During that same period, more than three-quarters of the ministry's senior officials were also discovered to have been former Nazis, a higher proportion than Hitler had appointed in those posts during the Third Reich. In the post-war years they formed a clique within the West German government and as such were able to protect their former comrades and continue promoting Nazi policies, including discrimination against homosexuals. During that same period just over half of the Interior Ministry staff were said to be ex-Party members, a number of them former employees of the Nazi Interior Ministry under *Reichsführer SS* Himmler.

The report further alleged that a number of these men

had 'participated in forced-sterilization programmes' and were people who 'today would have to be classified as Nazi perpetrators'. Although it was claimed that their presence had been 'tolerated rather than encouraged', Dr Frank Bösch, lead researcher for the report, stated: 'There was a belief that they were people who had done their duty in a difficult time.'

## Chapter Four

# REBUILDING AND REGENERATION

### The myth of the 'rubble women'

In the first weeks after Germany surrendered there was little sympathy for the population. The general feeling was that they had got what they deserved after supporting a regime which had decimated much of Europe and enslaved millions. Newsreel footage of the destruction of Berlin and other German cities left many unmoved as they remembered viewing similar scenes after the bombing of Warsaw, Rotterdam, Coventry and London.

But gradually the acrimony and resentment towards the German people diminished and some even felt a grudging respect for the ordinary women of Hamburg, Dresden and Berlin who cleared the debris brick by brick with their bare hands in preparation for the rebuilding of their devastated towns and cities. The iconic image of these so-called *Trümmerfrauen* (rubble women) working cheerfully among the ruins became symbolic of German resilience and helped restore pride to a defeated people, but it was a myth. These women were not all selfless volunteers as the majority were former Nazi Party members who had been forced to clear the rubble as part of their punishment. During the war the rubble-strewn streets and damaged buildings had been cleared by concentration camp inmates and slave labourers under guard in the aftermath of Allied bombing, often in hazardous conditions. It was therefore seen as reasonable punishment to compel the *Trümmerfrauen* to do likewise.

They were later joined by the unemployed, who worked in the ruins in return for extra food rations, and in some towns and cities by female university students who agreed to work for the right to enrol on a course. With most of the men in POW camps, it was left largely to the women to perform this task, but among the Allies only in the British zone were women employed in clearing the rubble. The French and Americans considered it too dangerous. Many buildings were unsafe and there were also lots of unexploded shells, mines and other hazards.

'Rubble women' form a human chain to clear bombed-out areas in the Russian sector of Berlin, July 1945.

The task was so enormous that it was necessary for the occupation authorities to make public appeals for volunteers, but contrary to popular perception these went largely unheeded and those who did volunteer were predominantly men. In Duisburg in the Ruhr, for example, only 50 of the 10,500 volunteers were women.

The myth of the *Trümmerfrauen* originated in West Berlin, where 26,000 women answered the appeal for volunteers, but in a city with half a million women of working age this amounted to just 5 per cent of the female workforce and the percentage of female volunteers in other German cities was significantly less.

In the Russian zone, there was greater parity as the population was encouraged to share the burden of reconstruction, as exemplified by a poster from the era depicting a young woman in overalls with a pick in one hand and a brick in the other. It carried the slogan: 'Every German Patriot Helps with the Rebuilding of Berlin.'

In the East, women were expected to join the labour force and contribute to a long-term regeneration programme, whereas in the West, German women were encouraged to return to their traditional role of homemaker as soon as the ruins had been cleared.

## Rubble mountains

Berlin is noted for its parks, forests, rivers and lakes and its mainly flat topography, but it also boasts three hills. The Kreuzberg is named after the national monument which crowns it; the Müggelberge is a ridge of wooded hills in the south-east of the city; and the Teufelsberg (Devil's Mountain) is a

260-foot-high (80 metres) man-made mound created entirely from the rubble of the Third Reich.

Carpet bombing by the Allies had levelled around 80 per cent of the capital's historic buildings, along with factories, schools, hospitals, libraries and of course tens of thousands of houses and apartment blocks. The same is true of other major cities in Germany, each of which has its own man-made rubble mountain – Leipzig has the 500-foot (153 metres) high Fockeberg, Frankfurt the Monte Scherbelino (Mount Shard) and Stuttgart the Grüner Heiner, to name but three.

West Germany alone had some 14 billion cubic feet of rubble to dispose of, sufficient to ring the entire country with a wall two metres thick and seven metres high.

After so much wanton and indiscriminate destruction it seems incredible that the first stage in rebuilding the country was to demolish a further 30 per cent of its largely undamaged historic buildings to make way for the new – a project which took the best part of 40 years to complete.

Of the 16 million apartments in Berlin, only ten million remained inhabitable. The urgency to house the surviving inhabitants and the millions of refugees who flooded into the city from the east necessitated the rushed construction of temporary accommodation. But the architects, developers and city planners also had to consider the long term.

## Restoration vs. modernization

There were plans to abandon the devastated cities and rebuild them nearby, but in many cases the surviving residents demanded that their old homes should be rebuilt and the character of their towns preserved. More was at stake than simply reconstruction. It was a highly emotive issue too. Should the new Germany be modernized and in doing so physically erase its past, or should the historic centres be restored to

Many German refugees, both civilian and military, ended up at Berlin's main station after being driven out of Poland and Czechoslovakia by the Allies, October 1945.

the state they had been in before Hitler brought ruin to the country? Would faithful reconstruction convey the impression that the nation had wilfully disregarded the Hitler years or would rebuilding in stone, steel and cement demonstrate that Germany was more forward-looking than at any single period in its history?

Ironically, the extensive destruction of Germany's major towns and cities enabled some of the architects and urban planners who had worked for the Third Reich to rebuild post-war Germany much as Hitler and his architect Albert Speer would have wished. After the war, the men who would have willingly laid waste to vast areas of Berlin to build Germania, Hitler's dream Third Reich capital, now resubmitted their plans to those entrusted with Germany's reconstruction. They dusted off their drawings dating from 1943 – when Speer had formed a working party to plan the modernization of Germany's major cities in anticipation of final victory over the Allies – and submitted them as if they were new.

The Hamburg architect Konstanty Gutschow was one of many who urged the development of 'structured and dispersed urban landscapes' of the type Hitler and Speer had envisaged, because they were more difficult to bomb than a densely populated and concentrated metropolis. Referring to Operation Gomorrah, the week-long Allied bombing campaign which flattened the city in July 1943, Gutschow said:

*This act of destruction will be a blessing. The Führer's prophesy that the ruined cities will rise again more resplendent than ever applies*

*doubly to Hamburg. We won't shed any tears*
*for the vast majority of destroyed buildings.*

Although Gutschow's allegiance to the Nazis prohibited him from being engaged in and profiting from post-war reconstruction, his old contacts ensured that he did not remain unemployed for long. Elsewhere, the same 'comrades' network' saw former Nazi-era architects, developers and construction firms with their snouts in the trough, benefitting financially from construction contracts. And there was no shortage of cash, thanks to the Marshall Plan and similar assistance schemes.

More than five million apartment blocks were built in West Germany in the first 15 years after the war, along with new roads, public buildings and housing developments.

The new suburbs and satellite towns were functional but sterile. Even Albert Speer's son, himself an architect, deplored the isolated ghetto-like residential developments and the featureless concrete public buildings, which one critic described as possessing 'garbage chute entrances'.

## Hearts and minds

*[The Third Reich constituted] 12 years of the rule of*
*bestiality, ignorance and illiteracy which brought about*
*the destruction of 2,000 years of German civilization.*
Richard Strauss, composer, 1 May 1945

In the summer and autumn of 1945, the Allies made a concerted effort to win the hearts and minds of ordinary Germans by sending over leading musicians and artists, such as Marlene Dietrich, Benjamin Britten and Yehudi Menuhin, to lift the spirits of a demoralized and dejected population.

On 27 July 1945, just three weeks after the liberation of Belsen, Britten and Menuhin performed for the former inmates, who were forced to remain in that wretched place while they recovered their health, but it was Britten and Menuhin who were most deeply moved by the occasion. Britten was so shaken by the experience that he refused to talk about it for many years and later confessed that everything he wrote subsequently had been influenced by it.

Menuhin, who had refused many invitations from conductor Wilhelm Furtwängler to perform with the Berlin Philharmonic in the interwar years, was the first Jewish musician of international standing to play there after the surrender, citing his hope to promote tolerance, to 'normalize' relations between former enemies and to rehabilitate German music. But his efforts at reconciliation met with protests from Jewish survivors. At a meeting with displaced persons, the violinist was asked by the editor of a Yiddish language newspaper to imagine what it was like for those who had lost several generations of their family in the camps.

*When you, the artist, see the ruins, you will say, 'What a pity that so much beauty has been destroyed.' When we, who have lost our families, see the same ruins, we shall say, 'What a pity that so much remained standing.'*

Prominent writers and intellectuals such as Ernest Hemingway, Rebecca West and George Orwell were also invited to visit

Germany and assess the impact of the war and its aftermath on a defeated people. They were responding to UNESCO's appeal for a concerted effort to begin the process of healing the German psyche.

## Failure to exorcize the past

Thomas Mann, formerly an émigré, was persuaded to return to renew Germany's 'morally mutilated soul' and on checking into a Bayreuth hotel discovered that the three previous signatures in the guest book belonged to Hitler, Himmler and Goebbels. He left the following 16 pages blank before signing in, one for each year of his exile. His adult children Erika and Klaus, who accompanied their father, were convinced that National Socialism had lost its populist appeal as a direct result of Germany's military defeats and not because the population had ceased to believe in its morally corrupt and criminal ideology. Mann later wrote of his reaction to receiving a gift of *People in the Making*, an old Nazi periodical from 1937, edited by a Nazi academic.

*It made distressing reading. I said to myself that it would not be easy to live among people who had been fed these drugs for 12 years. I said to myself that I would undoubtedly have many good and true friends over there: old and young. But also many lurking enemies – beaten enemies to be sure, but those are the worst, the most poisonous ...*

Klaus Mann would commit suicide in 1949 in a state of severe depression, largely caused by the disappointment he felt concerning the failed promise of post-war Germany to exorcize its past.

## An emotional return

For Mann's fellow émigrés, among them Marlene Dietrich and the film director Billy Wilder, it was an emotional return, tinged with a certain satisfaction in seeing that their warnings about endorsing a dictatorship, which few had heeded, had come to pass. Wilder had lost his mother and grandmother in the camps and had edited the harrowing Holocaust documentary *Death Mills*.

But having savoured that bitter-sweet sensation, they were now inclined to pity their former countrymen. They shared the idealistic belief that cultural renewal was possible, although one wonders what they imagined might be achieved by staging Shakespeare's *Measure for Measure*, or giving a concert of music by Purcell performed by the Cambridge Madrigal Society.

To their surprise and distress, some of these cultural ambassadors were more profoundly affected by their experiences than those whom they had come to scrutinize. Many returned drained and disillusioned, having seen that it was unfeasible to convince a 'brainwashed and starving nation' that they had been seized by a collective neurosis and that they alone were responsible for their predicament.

Others believed that the Germans were undeserving of compassion, that reconciliation was not possible and that the concentration camps offered sufficient evidence of this. But Orwell, who went as correspondent for *The Observer*, was among those who saw no merit in damning a defeated people with the burden of collective guilt and shared responsibility.

'To what extent can the simple peasants who troop to church on Sunday mornings be responsible for the horrors of Nazism?' he asked.

Of all those who made the trip in the first months of victory, it was Orwell who appeared the most concerned to understand the Nazi mindset and the appeal of the Germans' false messiah.

## Orwell's warning

Orwell discouraged the Allies from viewing Nazi Germany as something 'other' and urged them instead to see it as a social phenomenon that appealed to the emotions and to those who held certain personal beliefs, which would explain the growth of fascism outside Germany in the 1920s and 1930s. Hitler's personal appeal to his followers lay in his 'pathetic, dog-like face, the face of a man suffering under intolerable wrongs ... the martyr, the victim ... the self-sacrificing hero who fights single-handed against impossible odds'.

It was Orwell's contention that Hitler had been able to generate pity, fear, awe and even love in his adoring acolytes by making his minor accomplishments look like major triumphs and by portraying his weak and defenceless political adversaries as mighty foes. By doing so he was able to depict himself as struggling against apparently insurmountable odds and by that means elicit sympathy from those who felt that they too were at odds with an unjust world.

Orwell rejected the idea that the civilized world could always rely on reason to overcome the irrational and denied that fascism was alien to British culture. He warned against complacency and having blind faith in the inevitable progress of civilization, because the 'fascist streak' lies within us all, to some degree. Anxiety, insecurity and instability could lead to intolerance of other races and the persecution of those who could be used as a convenient scapegoat for current ills.

## Removing Nazi literature

But not all correspondents were as understanding or as forgiving. Ernest Hemingway and his then wife, the war correspondent Martha Gellhorn, painted the Germans as barbarians who had forfeited the right to be considered a civilized nation. Gellhorn said that after visiting Dachau she would never feel 'hope or innocence or gaiety again'.

Poet Stephen Spender could not rejoice in victory despite his experience of the London Blitz, when he had witnessed the suffering of his fellow Londoners. He remarked that 'even the German educated elite seemed unwilling to admit their culpability' and he despaired when he heard some of the British officers speak admiringly of their German counterparts who had fought for their country and of the émigrés as 'rats' who had deserted it.

Spender had been commissioned to oversee the removal of Nazi literature from booksellers and public libraries in the Ruhr and the Rhineland and found that the task was far simpler than he had imagined.

A librarian in Aachen told him:

*We understand exactly what you want, and there is no difficulty whatever about carrying out your instructions. You see, throughout the Nazi regime, we kept all the books by Jewish and socialist writers in a special cellar, under lock and key, as having only historical and scientific interest. All we have to do now is to take out these books and put them on our open shelves, while at the same time we lock up all the Nazi books, because now they only have historical and scientific interest.*

Other libraries had taken the initiative and disposed of the offending titles without encouragement or orders from the Allies.

## Rebecca West at Nuremberg

The novelist Rebecca West attended the Nuremberg trials and was not convinced that it was justice she was witnessing but rather a process of apportioning blame – a catharsis to exonerate the population from guilt.

In the 7 September issue of *The New Yorker*, she wrote of the judges:

*They all know very well that it is a pity that the defeated have to be tried by the victors, that it is impracticable to have judgment delivered by a neutral court. But they are all judges who know that every trial is flawed by the same imperfection, who are aware that every accused person is suffering the injustice of being tried by people who, in the economic and social struggles which have worsted him, have come off best, to the extent of being on the bench while he is in the dock. They believe that the imperfection can be remedied by strict adherence*

*to a code of law, which they must force themselves to*
*apply as if they were not victors but representatives of*
*a neutral power. One has read of such idealistic efforts*
*in history books. It is the charm of a visit to Nuremberg*
*that one sees the effort being made and, in listening*
*to arguments subtle as the serpent and slow as the*
*snail, counts the immense cost of legality and wonders*
*at the immense fortitude of those who are paying the*
*cost. For however much a man loved the law, he could*
*not love so much of it as lies about at Nuremberg.*

West found distraction from the 'tedious' process when she became romantically involved with a senior American judge, while Gellhorn and Dietrich both had affairs with US General James Gavin, commander of the 82nd Airborne Division. Gavin would provide the model for the hero of Billy Wilder's black comedy of the occupation, *A Foreign Affair*, in which Dietrich would star.

Dietrich herself enjoyed a love-hate relationship with the country of her birth, which she had renounced to take American citizenship. On returning to a war-ravaged Germany in 1945, she told a journalist, 'I guess Germany deserves everything that's coming to her', while making a distinction between being anti-Nazi and anti-German. She asked to be taken to Belsen, where she believed her sister Liesel (Elisabeth) had been interned, but was sickened to learn that Liesel and her husband had collaborated with the Nazis and were living in style near the camp. From that day on she denied she had ever had a sister.

## Intellectual emissaries

Author Evelyn Waugh interpreted the invitation to tour the country as an endorsement of his own cultural importance, referring to himself as 'the first major poet to fly the Atlantic'. While there, he lived the life of a debauched Roman emperor, with a handsome personal chef he had picked up and a supply of looted wine. He saw the proceedings in Nuremberg as a tragedy enacted by a cast of second-rate personalities and was unimpressed by the defendants, describing Goering as a 'matron' and Ribbentrop as 'a seedy schoolmaster'.

Others found they couldn't function after viewing the camps.

The writer and philosopher Hannah Arendt, who coined the phrase 'the banality of evil' to describe the Nazi functionaries, observed:

*Everywhere one notices that there is no reaction to what has happened, but it is hard to say whether that is due to an intentional refusal to mourn, or whether it is the expression of a genuine emotional incapacity.*

Lee Miller, the combat photojournalist, took a bath in Hitler's private tub at the 'airless, poky and drab' Munich apartment he had shared with his mistress, Eva Braun. That morning, 29 April, she had been with the Americans who liberated Dachau. Of that famous picture her son would later say:

*I think she was sticking two fingers up at Hitler. On the floor are her boots, covered with the filth of Dachau, which she has trodden all over Hitler's bathroom floor.*

*She is saying she is the victor. But what she didn't know was that a few hours later in Berlin, Hitler and Eva Braun would kill themselves in his bunker.*

Miller would later blame the sights she had witnessed at Dachau and Buchenwald as contributing to her alcoholism and clinical depression.

But although these intellectual emissaries were accused of participating in little more than a public relations exercise, there were serious efforts made by the Allies to contribute to the regeneration of German culture. Peter de Mendelssohn, press officer for the British Control Commission, was

American photographer Lee Miller bathes in the bathroom of Adolf Hitler's house in Munich, 1945. Her combat boots are on the floor.

entrusted with verifying the credentials of German journalists and organizing a free press in the British zone (*Der Spiegel* and *Die Welt* were considered reliable by their German readership). Equally significant was the contribution made by progressive educator Robert Birley, future headmaster of Eton, who reformed and restructured the German educational system. Literacy, numeracy and the core subjects had all been fatally neglected during the Hitler years, as National Socialist indoctrination took priority over the basic curriculum, leaving a generation semi-literate and woefully ill-informed. Both men arguably did more in the long term to revive the country than these flying visits by highbrow celebrities.

## *Trümmerfilme* (Rubble Films)

'This film was shot in Berlin in the summer of 1947. It is intended to be simply an objective, true-to-life picture of this enormous, half-destroyed city, in which three and a half million people are carrying on a frightful, desperate existence almost without realizing it. They live in tragedy as if it were their natural element, but out of exhaustion, not through strength of mind or faith. This film is not an accusation against the German people, nor yet a defence of them. It is simply a presentation of the facts. But if anyone who has seen the story of Edmund Koehler comes to realize that something must be done, that German children must be taught to love life again, then the efforts of those who made this film will have been amply rewarded.'

Roberto Rossellini, *Germany, Year Zero*, 1948

The spate of American- and European-funded films made in Germany in the immediate post-war years by Billy Wilder, Jacques Tourneur (*Berlin Express*), Howard Hawks (*I Was a Male War Bride*) and Fred Zinnemann (*The Search*) did not come into being out of altruism. Hollywood's cash assets in Europe had been frozen when the war started and they could only be released if they were spent on productions filmed in the country where the cash had been deposited.

It would be left to German filmmakers working under the Soviet-sponsored DEFA production company to dissect and address the serious implications and repercussions of the Hitler years (although Rossellini's neorealist *Germany, Year Zero* was a notable exception). The British and Americans were concerned only with producing entertainment, not re-educating the Germans.

That duty was entrusted to the short series of social realist films funded by DEFA between 1946 and 1950, which came to be known as *Trümmerfilme* (Rubble Films), and though they found favour with foreign critics and audiences the domestic audience was understandably reluctant to pay to see on the big screen the devastation and privations that they were confronted with every day.

Wolfgang Staudte's *The Murderers Are Among Us* (1946) betrayed the difficulty the Germans had in confronting their past. The female lead plays a camp survivor with an unrealistically optimistic outlook on life and no physical signs of having suffered from maltreatment, sickness or starvation. She appears to have walked out of the camp in full make-up and with an immaculate and fashionable hairdo, presumably having been imprisoned with her personal stylist.

'One might have expected a spiritual vacuum to follow the collapse of the Third Reich and of the ideologies which had spawned it, but this did not happen. The other Germany, though buried under the pressures of the totalitarian regime, had not fossilised. Freed from the dead-weight of the past, it surfaced again in 1945, slowly at first, but then, with the support of the Western Allies, at ever-increasing pace. That was the true post-war "German miracle" and it first came to pass in the Berlin of the Golden Hunger Years.'

George Clare, *Berlin Days*

## A free press

*What is necessary is that the press blindly follow the basic principle: the leadership is always right!*
Hitler in a speech to journalists, 10 November 1938

During the Hitler years, free speech was stifled, German and Austrian journalists were gagged and even foreign correspondents were subject to censorship by Goebbels' Ministry of Public Enlightenment and Propaganda. Those correspondents who criticized the dictatorship in print risked having their press passes revoked, while German and Austrian nationals lived in fear of being thrown into a concentration camp.

As General Keitel remarked at Nuremberg in defence of the 'Night and Fog' ('*Nacht und Nebel*') decree, which legalized internment without trial: 'Efficient intimidation can only be achieved either by capital punishment or by measures by which the relatives of the criminal and the population do not know his fate.'

For 12 years, Germany's journalists were no more than mouthpieces for the regime. They were vetted by the state-controlled press agency, the DNB (*Deutsches Nachrichtenbüro* – the German news bureau), and every serious piece written for radio, newspapers and magazines had to be submitted to the DNB for approval.

Inevitably, the end of the war saw a proliferation of new publications – 150 of them appeared in the first three years of peace. A small number of these were printed in Yiddish, serving as a lifeline for the 15,000 German Jews who had survived the Holocaust. The editors of the titles sponsored by the Allies were instructed not to print anything that might suggest there was friction between the Four Powers, but the 'Amis' couldn't have it both ways. If they advocated a free press they would have to tolerate criticism, justified or not.

Newspapers such as *Der Ruf* employed young journalists who

vilified the American occupation forces and accused the new American-funded radio stations (RIAS and Radio Liberty) of peddling propaganda, but reading the uncensored views of the more articulate members of the population proved instructive to those in the Allied administration, who were prepared to listen and to learn from them. Among the lessons they learned from the new German press were that restrictive measures on their own only brought resentment and that imposing democracy was counterproductive. The only political structures that had a chance of outliving the occupation had to be established by the Germans themselves, with the consent of the majority of the citizens. Imposing martial law, purging public life of former Nazis and pouring money into the economy would neither guarantee the regeneration of Germany nor its prosperity or future stability.

## Art for art's sake

The Nazis had attempted to eradicate everything they considered un-German. They banned music by Jewish composers (Mendelssohn, Mahler and Schoenberg), reviled composers who had opposed the regime (Alban Berg) and prohibited the performance of jazz ('*Negermusik*'), as well as music they had condemned as uncivilized or indecent (that of Stravinsky or Hindemith). They also held so-called 'degenerate art' ('*Entartete Kunst*') up to ridicule, although an exhibition of seized works staged in Munich in 1937, which was intended to inspire revulsion, attracted two million visitors, four times as many as the Nazi-approved art exhibition next door. Even if a proportion of those who filed past the paintings attended out of idle curiosity, it was evident that a large section of the population did not share the views of the dictatorship. It was, therefore, imperative that one aspect of the denazification process should be the cultural re-education of the population and the encouragement of those German artists who were keen to refute the philistine philosophy promulgated by the Nazi 'culture' ministry under Goebbels.

As if in answer to 12 years of cultural nihilism, artists such as Arnold Bode produced some of the most experimental and provocative art of the post-war years. In 1955 Bode established the 100-day-long international exhibition 'Documenta' in Kassel to rebut the country's Nazi past and establish a new cultural voice.

Some of Germany's most radical and influential artists of the post-war period, such as performance artist Joseph Beuys, a former member of the Hitler Youth, had experienced the negativism of National Socialist policy towards the arts at first hand and their subsequent rejection of it demonstrated their desire to dissociate themselves from their past.

Conceptual artists Bernd and Hilla Becher took photographs of desolate industrial landscapes (which they termed 'anonymous sculptures') as a direct response to being raised in the bombed wasteland of Düsseldorf, in contrast to the explosion of abstract art exemplified by Willi Baumeister and Ernst Wilhelm Nay, who presented mythic, primordial forms which saved the artists and the viewers from having to confront the recent past.

Inevitably, there was a revival of German expressionism by the likes of Markus Lüpertz and Anselm Kiefer, who referenced Nazi propaganda and the art of the Weimar years associated with Otto Dix and George Grosz, whom the Nazis had categorized as 'degenerate'.

## Restitution

The punishment of Nazi war criminals understandably took precedence over restitution. The return of the property looted during 12 years of Nazi 'Aryanization' was considered to be a long-term aim and one that was fraught with difficulties, the main one being the fact that many of the owners were dead, making their fate extremely difficult, if not impossible, to verify. But an effort had to be made and this was the unenviable task entrusted to the Allied Control Council in Berlin, which had the authority to pursue such matters in all four zones.

It was not only Jews, of course, who had lost their assets, businesses, family heirlooms, art treasures and personal valuables, but also the national museums, galleries and libraries of the occupied countries. Their priceless collections had been plundered and as much as possible needed to be recovered to restore national pride. But the Russians had little interest in returning valuable property to its rightful owners, especially those items that had belonged to Jews, and were more interested in shipping whatever treasures and assets they could recover back to Russia. This included entire industrial plants and factories, which were dismantled, as well as countless tons of mineral resources and even the contents of Austria's oil wells and refineries.

The Russians justified the seizure of what they determined to be German assets and capital under the pretext that these were taken in lieu of reparations, but in doing so they also stripped Austria, Hungary, Bulgaria, Yugoslavia, Romania, Poland and Finland of their national assets and resources. This indiscriminate process appeared to be nothing more than Aryanization in reverse and it is likely that much of this plunder (amounting to a staggering 1.5 billion dollars' worth in Austria, plus 188 million dollars' worth in the Balkans and Eastern Europe) had never been German. Concerns were raised by the French, British and Americans, but their protests were purely political because they all knew the risk they ran by angering the Soviets. Besides, the British had little sympathy for the Austrians, whom they saw as Germans with slightly different accents.

## The fate of the Jews

*We do not want revenge. If we took this*
*vengeance it would mean we would fall to*
*the depths and ethics and morals the German*
*nation has been in these past ten years.*
Dr Zalman Grinberg speaking at Dachau, May 1945

It could be argued that the Holocaust was largely in response to one man's neurotic obsession with purging Europe of a people on whom he projected his own psychosis. As the American psychoanalyst Walter C. Langer observed: 'The Jew became a symbol of everything Hitler hated in himself.'

Ironically, one of the consequences of Nazi persecution was to increase interest in Judaism among many who had renounced their religion in the 1920s and 1930s in anticipation of becoming assimilated into German society. The rate of intermarriage between Jews and Gentiles was so high in the interwar years that it was thought that almost all Austrian and German Jews would have been assimilated by the millennium had there been no Holocaust.

After the camps were liberated, incidents of anti-Semitism were rare, although when they occurred they betrayed the old prejudices and revived racial stereotypes. They were not confined to German civilians. In Kielce, in central Poland, 42 Jews were massacred and more than 80 seriously injured after an eight-year-old boy falsely accused the town's Jews of abducting him and other children. Thirty more were murdered that day in isolated incidents in the vicinity. In Hungary, Poland and Slovakia, as many as 1,500 Jews were murdered in the first year of peace, while many Jews who had fought with the partisans in other Eastern European countries were set upon and killed by their neighbours after returning to their homes.

Holocaust survivor Michael Etkind was warned not to return to his home in Poland: 'The Poles are killing all the Jews returning from the camps.' And in Bad Ischl in Austria locals formed a lynch mob to throw stones and shout abuse when they learned that the former camp inmates were being given larger rations. But for their part, the Jews had no heart for revenge against the German and Austrian people – only against those individuals who were guilty of murdering their families.

In *Safe Among the Germans: Liberated Jews After World War II* (2002), author Ruth Gay reveals that there had been one isolated incident when a group of former inmates planned to poison the drinking water in Nuremberg, but were prevented by future Israeli prime minister David Ben-Gurion. They then pressed ahead with plans to poison the bread fed to German POWs, but none of their intended victims died.

The Nazis had been heard attempting to justify their mass murder of the Jews by arguing that if the boot had been on the other foot the Jews would have massacred them, but this was Nazi neurosis and doublethink gone mad. On the contrary, after the war there were many Jews who felt nothing but pity for the ordinary Germans suffering privation and viewed them as fellow human beings.

It was due to the efforts of individual Jews, such as the publisher Victor Gollancz, that Red Cross parcels were finally distributed in the American zone in the spring of 1946, after having been initially sent to other parts of Europe that were felt more deserving of aid. Field Marshal Montgomery had argued that three-quarters of the German population were and remained ardent Nazis and should be starved into seeing sense. However, Gollancz, a German émigré whose family had been persecuted by the Nazis, argued that all combatant nations had committed shameful acts, so the Allies had no right to condemn the Germans to further suffering. In addition, it would only reinforce their resentment and encourage future conflict.

*I feel called upon to help suffering Germans precisely because I am a Jew ... we are starving them, not deliberately in the sense that we want them to die, but wilfully in the sense that we prefer their death to our own inconvenience.*

# Repatriation of ethnic Germans

In the turmoil that attended the first weeks and months of peace, much was done out of necessity that was later regretted and nothing more so, perhaps, than the forced expulsion of up to 14 million ethnic Germans from Eastern Europe.

The German-speaking population of Hungary, Poland and Czechoslovakia were driven from their homes by the Allies and transported under deplorable conditions to Germany, which was in no fit state to receive them. It has been estimated that somewhere between 500,000 and one and a half million may have died in the internment camps or on the journey, either from starvation, disease or neglect.

It was a tragedy that has been neglected by historians – it has been accorded no more than a footnote if mentioned at all – and it is all the more deplorable because it need never have happened.

It could be argued that it had been planned with the best intentions. The ethnic Germans were thought to have been at risk of reprisals from the local inhabitants of those countries because of the countless atrocities committed by the SS *Einsatzgruppen* murder squads and by rogue units of the Wehrmacht.

It was also believed that their neighbours might attack anyone of German origin merely because they had suffered enough under the Nazi yoke.

Hitler had exploited what he presented as being the vulnerability of German minorities in neighbouring states in order to justify invasion, so these communities were seen as satellite states of the Third Reich by many politicians and military leaders after Germany's capitulation. In some quarters, they were considered a potential threat to future peace and were even seen as an enclave of aggrieved nascent Nazis.

## Polish vengeance

The Poles were unapologetic. General Karol Świerczewski, commander of the Polish Second Army, told his men:

*We are behaving with the Germans as they behaved with us. Many have already forgotten how they treated our children, women and old people ... One must perform one's task in such a harsh and decisive manner that the German vermin do not hide in their houses but rather will flee from us of their own volition ... and will thank God that they were lucky enough to save their heads.*

Their hunger for vengeance was understandable. Whole communities had been eradicated and generations of the same family had been wiped out in a single *Aktion*, as the Germans called them.

Hundreds of thousands of Poles had been evicted from their homes, farms and businesses on Hitler's orders and their property and possessions handed over to ethnic Germans, so the Allies imagined that they were simply expelling these 'settlers' and restoring order. But only a small proportion, approximately three-quarters of a million, of those expelled by the Allies had been used by Hitler in this way.

In 1945 they joined a stream of 'settlers' who had been driven out by partisans and followed the westward migration of ethnic Germans who had abandoned their homes in the Black

Sea region, Ukraine, Romania and Yugoslavia in fear of the approaching Red Army. So it is not entirely true that all of the ethnic Germans had been forced at gunpoint by the Allies to abandon the homes they had seized from the original owners with Hitler's approval.

Their haste was accelerated by rumours of atrocities perpetrated by vengeful Czechs at Brno, where more than 300 ethnic Germans had been killed and others publicly tortured to death. There were rumours too of 28,000 ethnic Germans having been rounded up and marched to the Austrian border, where they were detained indefinitely in overcrowded, insanitary conditions. According to Lieutenant Colonel Byford-Jones:

*When I saw their passport pictures, taken a few months before, I was staggered. The change these people had undergone was incredible. They had all lost weight, aged ten years, had lined faces. They were sick and mentally unbalanced ...*

*I went round some of the refugee camps – former barracks, schools, quarantine stations, Red Cross centres – which were like a crown of thorns round the festering head of Berlin – and I saw such human degradation, depravity and tragedy that I was physically sick after a few hours of it ...*

## Suffering of migrants

The expulsions had been considered as early as the spring of 1942 and it had been explicitly stated at the Potsdam Conference in August 1945 that they were to be carried out in an 'orderly and humane fashion'. However, the scale of the operation was simply too much for the Allies to handle at that time and with the resources they could spare in the chaotic conditions that existed in post-war Europe. The British Foreign Office had stipulated that it would take up to a decade to repatriate that amount of people, if the road and rail networks were not to be congested with expellees, but the Allies were not able to set aside the resources needed over such a timescale. They needed to relocate the ethnic Germans while they still had sufficient troops to supervise the expulsions.

There were those who warned the Allies that they were courting disaster. George Orwell foresaw an 'enormous crime equivalent to transplanting the entire population of Australia', but this was dismissed as alarmist. The Allies did not have much time for the Germans and were more concerned not to be seen as weak or forgiving. Any misgivings were disregarded as overly pessimistic.

Unfortunately, it would necessitate using what the Foreign Office described as 'concentration camps' to house them until adequate provision could be made for their resettlement. The use of such an emotive term would later be seized upon by Nazi apologists to imply that these German civilians had suffered as much as the Jews under Hitler. And there was evidence that the overcrowded transports bringing these Germans back to the Fatherland were reminiscent of scenes witnessed by Allied troops at the liberation of the camps. As one British soldier remarked: 'The removal of the dead in carts from the railway stations was a grim reminder of what I saw in Belsen.'

Many of the expellees had lived in the East for generations and were forced to leave their homes with no more than they could carry. It is alleged that they were denied water, food and winter clothing on the journey, which saw many die from malnutrition and hypothermia.

Such was the suffering experienced by these unwilling migrants that the Allied Control Council called for the operation to cease in the winter of 1947. Whatever the justification offered, it was undeniably a shameful episode and one that tainted the record of the Allied occupation of Germany.

## War child

*Hitler is now forgotten and the sterile philosophy with which he caused such turmoil has perished with him ... Of the documents that bear witness to the psychic power which he exercised little is left but the impression of his voice, which arouses in the survivors a feeling of embarrassment rather than fascination.*
Joachim Fest, *The Face of the Third Reich*

Long after the physical evidence of National Socialism and its symbols had been removed from public buildings and the ruins of the Third Reich cleared and built upon, the trauma of those years remained. A generation of children who had lived through the war grew up haunted by memories they had unconsciously suppressed. Some were even haunted by memories they had acquired from their parents and grandparents, who refused to talk about those times, but who conveyed their experiences in other ways without meaning to.

Alexandra Senfft, the granddaughter of a Nazi war criminal and the author of a foreword to *Kriegskinder*, a book of childhood memories of the Second World War says:

*What the* Kriegskinder *did not come to terms with they passed on to us grandchildren. Psychologists have found that many grandchildren internalized their grandparents' experience even if the Nazi era was never spoken of. Grandchildren thus often possess the family memory without having experienced the events themselves.*

War child and psychoanalyst Hartmut Radebold confirmed this in an interview with *Der Spiegel* on 28 March 2013:

*Many children have unconsciously adopted the symptoms of their parents. One patient dreams of the tank attacks that his father experienced. The adults have conveyed much more through gestures and insinuations than they realize. This has been absorbed by the children and incorporated into their identities. Parents unconsciously pass on tasks to their children: Carry on with the family, do a better job and protect us, so we don't decompensate.*

Radebold, who was nine years old when the Russians laid siege to Berlin, said he witnessed 'everything imaginable'. His own mother became 'emotionally paralyzed' on hearing of her husband's death and never cried again and his 15-year-old brother was abducted by the Russians and sent to a labour camp. When he returned two years later he was seriously ill and suffered from 'hunger swelling', which gave him a distended stomach. People would ask him where he had found so much food to make him fat.

Having researched traumatic war experiences, Radebold concluded that the unconscious has no sense of time, and so knowing that such experiences happened a long time ago does not alleviate the trauma. It can resurface at any time and it is experienced as vividly as if it was happening in the present.

In the 1970s, Radebold treated patients whose symptoms originated with their wartime experiences, but at that time the war was still a taboo subject for many, and so psychoanalysts could not always ask the right questions. Predictably those responsible for war crimes did not feel the need to seek treatment as they presumably felt no twinges of conscience, although some of the children of these perpetrators did seek help. But for Germans of that generation psychoanalysis was suspect because they considered it to be a Jewish science.

## Raped by the Russians

Time did not heal the emotional scars of the women who had been raped by the Russians after the fall of Berlin. And their plight was not helped by the fact that the very subject was considered to be taboo for decades.

Eighty-year-old Ruth Schumacher did not speak about, or even dare to think about, her experiences for over 60 years until a German university study brought the subject to the surface. She was 18 years old when she was dragged from the waterlogged mine in the East German town of Halle-Bruckdorf, where she and dozens of her neighbours had taken shelter from the shelling. She was then repeatedly raped.

'I was gang-raped by five Russians,' she told an American radio station in 2009. 'You can never forget something like that. The study has been helpful, but of course it brought back everything. And I've had a lot of sleepless nights because of it.'

When the Russians occupied the region, the Communist authorities compelled the victims to sign a statement denying that their troops had participated in sexual assaults on civilians. They wanted the Red Army to be remembered as heroes and not barbarians. The fear of what might happen to them and their families if they spoke out, mingled with the shame and the guilt, led many women to suppress their memories until recently.

The author of the study, Dr Philipp Kuwert of the University of Greifswald, believed that it was important for the victims to be able to speak about their ordeal. 'Even a late voice is better than no voice at all,' he said.

But he was adamant that the study was not an attempt to diminish what the German troops had done to women in the concentration camps and the conquered territories.

'The German troops committed a lot of rapes, mainly in Eastern Europe. And of course there was a lot of sexualized violence in the concentration camps. I find it very important to mention that.'

Even after the break-up of the USSR, the Russians still dismiss the mass rape of German women as a myth or anti-Soviet propaganda, although the documented evidence is overwhelming. One of the best-known examples is the unpublished diary of a young Jewish Ukrainian lieutenant, Vladimir Gelfand, who participated in the battle for Berlin. On 25 April he came upon a group of German women carrying suitcases. They told him that they had been repeatedly raped. One of the younger girls had been raped by 20 Russians in one night in front of her mother and she now begged Gelfand to sleep with her, to do as he wished, but to protect her.

It was a pitiable story, but the lieutenant knew that the Wehrmacht had also raped women and murdered children in every village during their four-year occupation of Russia, despite claiming to be an elite Aryan race of supermen who were forbidden to have sex with 'inferior races'.

It has been argued that the superhuman effort expended by the Germans after the war to rebuild the country and the economy was partly an effort to assuage their collective guilt and partly to avoid having to face the trauma of what they had recently experienced.

*Nothing is so unworthy of a civilized nation as allowing itself to be governed without opposition by an irresponsible clique that has yielded to base instinct. It is certain that today every honest German is ashamed of his government. Who among us has any conception of the dimensions of shame that will befall us and our children when one day the veil has fallen from our eyes and the most horrible of crimes – crimes that infinitely outdistance every human measure – reach the light of day?*
First Leaflet, White Rose anti-Nazi
resistance group, June 1942

## Daughter of a monster

Helga Schneider was four years old when her mother, Traudi, turned her back on her and her baby brother to join the SS. It was 1942 and 30 years were to pass before Helga saw her again, during which time she and her brother were raised by an abusive stepmother and suffered a succession of traumatic experiences which were to leave her emotionally scarred for life. When she finally tracked Traudi down, the 60-year-old woman had returned to her birthplace, Vienna, and was demonstrably proud of having served as a concentration camp guard at Auschwitz-Birkenau, where 12,000 men, women and children were murdered every day. She invited her daughter to try on her old uniform and offered her a handful of jewellery stolen from her victims.

*After 30 years I had in front of me, not a mother, but a war criminal. And one who was not penitent. One who still said it was right. I always recall a phrase she used about the old days: in German, 'Es war so schön', it was so beautiful! Nazism was so beautiful! She was always repeating this phrase ... That was her life, she was still in agreement with it. Still a Nazi. Still convinced that it was a righteous cause.*

Helga made her excuses and left, telling herself that she had no mother now and never had. Her own son would never know his maternal grandmother and it was better that he did not have one than live with the shame of having a convicted murderer in his family (Traudi had been found guilty at one of the subsequent Nuremberg trials).

Then in 1988 Helga was persuaded to visit her mother one last time. Traudi was senile and it might be the last chance for a reconciliation.

*I thought, let's see, perhaps she has repented at last. Perhaps she's realized she got everything wrong: the Nazi ideology, her fanaticism, the fact that she sacrificed everything for that ideology. She's old, thin – unbelievably fragile. She can't weigh more than seven stone. A woman who, 27 years ago, was still a healthy, vigorous, robust woman. I can't suppress a feeling of infinite pity.*

But to her dismay Traudi still took 'profound pleasure' in recalling the cruelty she had meted out to those who had been at her mercy. One inmate had attempted to save his daughter by reminding Traudi that he had once been in business with her father, but Traudi showed no pity.

*I had orders to treat [the prisoners] with extreme harshness and I made them spit blood.*

*What? Did I support the Final Solution? Why do you think I was there? For a holiday?*

*Not everyone died [in the gas chambers] at the same rate ... Newborn babies took only a few minutes; they pulled out some that were literally electric blue ...*

*The fourth crematorium in Birkenau had no ovens ...*
*because it was never finished. All it had was a big*
*well filled with hot embers ... The new commander in*
*Auschwitz found it terribly amusing. He used to line*
*the prisoners up on the edge of the well and then*
*have them shot, to enjoy the scene as they fell in ...*

Helga never saw her mother again, but the memory of her laughter while she recounted her stories of camp life generated nightmares from which she would wake in a cold sweat, her heart racing. There was only one way to exorcize the demon – to write about it. And only by doing that was Helga finally able to banish the oppressive shadow.

But in recording the suffering of Germans during the Hitler years and seeking to compare this to the brutality inflicted upon the victims of the regime, there is what historian Nicholas Stargardt calls:

*... the danger of making facile moral and political*
*comparisons between all the groups of people*
*who suffered in the war and the Holocaust ... There*
*can be no comparison between the events of the*
*Holocaust and the war which German families*
*had lived through. There can be no cancellation*
*of one horror by invoking another, although this*
*was just what much of the public discussion in*
*Germany in the early 1950s strove to effect.*

## Cold War

*From Stettin in the Baltic to Trieste in the Adriatic an
'Iron Curtain' has descended across the continent.
Behind that lie all the capitals of the ancient states of
Central Europe and Eastern Europe. Warsaw, Berlin,
Prague, Vienna, Budapest, Belgrade, Bucharest and
Sofia; all these famous cities and the populations
around them lie in what I must call the Soviet sphere,
and all are subject, in one form or another, not only
to Soviet influence but to a very high and in some
cases increasing measure of control from Moscow.*
Winston Churchill, 1946

Few who watched the staged newsreel footage of the historic meeting between the advance units of the American and Soviet armies at Torgau on the Elbe on 25 April would have been taken in by the affected camaraderie. Hitler himself had clung to the fatally optimistic belief that the Russians and the Americans would turn on each other at the last critical moment, forcing the Americans to form an uneasy alliance with Nazi Germany to forestall the 'red menace'. In that he was clearly deluded, but the capitalist democracies and Communist Russia were natural enemies straining at the leash to secure dominion over Europe.

In the immediate aftermath of the battle for Berlin, the city was occupied by the Soviets, but Stalin had earlier agreed to turn over some of the sectors to his former allies and in July the Russians withdrew from them. The four zones were then administered by the Allied Control Council, with each member nation taking control in turn. But governing the divided country and establishing common policy and authority often took second place to accommodating the Russians.

Stalinist Russia was seen as a serious threat to world stability as it continued to expand its influence in the immediate post-war years, while the Allies were preoccupied with the transition from war to peace. In addition to establishing Soviet satellite states in Eastern Europe, the Russians were enlarging their empire by backing Chinese communists in their civil war against the nationalists. It was also feared that Soviet nuclear tests would lead to the Russians stockpiling an arsenal of atomic bombs and long-range missiles, thereby posing a threat to the United States as well as Europe.

Major arterial roads in West Germany were already being planted with mines in anticipation of a surprise Soviet invasion but the first real test of the West's resolve to resist Russian expansion came in 1948, with Stalin's order to put a blockade around Berlin, a tactic the Russian dictator hoped would lead to the Allies withdrawing from the city. However, to Stalin's dismay, the Allies were able to circumvent the blockade by flying in supplies to the besieged Berliners, a lifeline they could have maintained indefinitely.

Konrad Adenauer was the first chancellor of West Germany. A former prisoner of the Nazis, he had been appointed as mayor of Berlin in May 1945 but was dismissed by the British for complaining about the lack of food. He then founded a new political party, the Christian Democratic Union, which was grounded on socialist principles but pitted itself against its socialist rivals. Adenauer was convinced that the survival of the new West German government depended on its cooperation with Britain, France and the United States.

Ironically, his Communist counterpart in East Germany was also a former anti-Nazi. Walter Ulbricht escaped to Russia during the Hitler years and became a stalwart supporter of Joseph Stalin. He then returned to Germany in 1945 to head the new Socialist Unity Party, lobbying for reform and independence from the Soviet bloc while at the same time advocating the building of the Berlin Wall. He blamed,

*... the 10 million Germans who in 1932 cast their votes for Hitler in free elections, although we Communists warned that 'He who votes for Hitler, votes for war.' ... The tragedy of the German people consists of the fact that they obeyed a band of gangsters.*

The Communist state ensured East Germans would not make the same mistake again by depriving them of the right to vote.

## Divide and conquer

In 1949, West and East Germany were formally divided into two separate states. The Federal Republic of West Germany came into being on 23 May and East Germany, or the DDR (Deutsche Demokratische Republik), on 7 October. From that day onwards, the leadership of the DDR claimed to be the only legal German state and refused to acknowledge the existence of the other half of the country. West Germany only became an independent sovereign state six years later when it joined NATO after signing

◇

As part of the propaganda war between East and West, a Soviet-inspired banner was unfurled next to the Russian–American Berlin Border, May 1949. It says in German: 'The Sector of Freedom welcomes the fighters for freedom and justice of the western sectors.'

the North Atlantic Treaty and was publicly recognized as 'the only German government freely and legitimately constituted and therefore entitled to speak for Germany as the representative of the German people in international affairs'.

In the interim, Stalin suggested a solution to the political impasse which would involve the reunification of Germany as a neutral state, but the Western Allies dismissed his assurances that the USSR would respect German neutrality. They were also extremely wary of allowing a reunified Germany to rearm, which it would need to do if it was to defend itself against its neighbours.

In 1952 the DDR erected a permanent barrier across the entire length of the internal East–West German border, consisting of barbed wire, minefields, manned watchtowers and deadly automatic machine gun traps, which were triggered by movement sensors. This 858-mile-long belt claimed the lives of an estimated 700 East Germans, in addition to those who died attempting the deadly crossing from East to West Berlin.

East Germany was now effectively the buffer state that Stalin claimed he needed to ensure the security of the Soviet Union. Together with Czechoslovakia, Poland, Romania, Hungary and Bulgaria, Russian-occupied East Germany formed not only an impregnable defensive border but also provided a rich vein of natural resources and industrial facilities to be plundered by the mother state.

For the population of what was now the German Democratic Republic there would be a severe restriction of freedom of movement and of speech, together with other severe restrictions and impositions that denied them their basic human rights.

Practically every aspect of life in the GDR was now overseen by a faceless bureaucracy and every citizen was made aware that they were under constant surveillance. They had merely exchanged one dictatorship for another. The fascist totalitarian regime of Adolf Hitler had been superseded by the Communist authoritarian administration under 'Uncle Joe' Stalin, which was equally brutal and employed the State Security Service to enforce its draconian laws.

The *Staatssicherheitsdienst*, commonly known as the Stasi, was a plain-clothes police force which was feared as much as the Gestapo had been and it used similar methods including torture, intimidation, blackmail and murder to keep the population under control. The eyes of the Stasi were everywhere and their ranks were augmented by 'unofficial employees' – paid informants recruited from the general population, who were feared and despised. Anyone could be working for the secret police.

But contrary to expectations, the Stasi were not interested in finding rank and file party members who had attempted to find anonymity in the GDR.

Dieter Skiba, a department leader in the Ministry for State Security, told Malte Herwig:

*NSDAP membership alone wasn't relevant to us ... For us, members of the NSDAP or the Hitler Youth and so on weren't the kind of Nazis we were interested in ... Our definition of a Nazi wasn't about membership of the NSDAP, but the role someone played during the era of fascism.*

## 1984

The euphemistically named German Democratic Republic was anything but. It was, in fact, George Orwell's dystopian world of doublespeak and terror, described in his novel *1984*, made manifest.

Families and friends were divided, many never to see each other again. In Berlin the absurdity as well as the cruelty of the situation was made tangible by the presence of the barriers, sentry posts and warning signs which divided the French, British and American zones from the Russian zone and which would become all the more substantial with the building of the Wall in 1961.

In one part of the city, the houses on one side of the street were allocated to the Soviet zone while those on the opposite side were given to the Allies. The residents on the south side of Bernauer Strasse found themselves under the ever-watchful eye of the Russians, while the pavement and the street itself was controlled by the French. As a consequence, some sections of Berlin were to benefit from the Marshall Plan and enjoy all the luxuries offered by a capitalist society, while their neighbours across the street looked on with envy like prisoners behind barbed wire.

The situation was made all the more farcical by the fact that Berlin was now an urban island 100 miles inside the GDR. To reach it, visitors from West Germany would have to either fly in or drive down a corridor (the old Führer autobahn) overlooked by manned watchtowers; they were forbidden from stopping during the entire four-hour journey, with the exception of one official refuelling stop. When they got there, travellers from the

Barbed wire tops the early version of the Berlin Wall; building began in 1961 to stop East Germans migrating to the West.

West would be advised not to produce more money than was needed to pay for petrol and refreshments, for fear of offending the poorly paid East German cashiers.

## Soviet propaganda

The East German population were continually bombarded with Communist propaganda, one of the most flagrant examples being *The Agitator's Notebook*. This notorious document was published by the Socialist Unity Party's Agitation Department in November 1955 and contained the following warning to would-be defectors:

*... leaving the GDR is an act of political and moral backwardness and depravity ... Is it not despicable when for the sake of a few alluring job offers or other false promises about a 'guaranteed future' one leaves a country in which the seed of a new and more beautiful life is sprouting ... for the place that favours a new war and destruction?*

It went on to accuse those who had left, or were considering leaving, the GDR of betraying the people who had laboured for a better future. By choosing to work for the American and British secret services, the West German industrialists and warmongering militarists, they became traitors.

## Brutal repression

Even those who reluctantly accepted their lot were soon feeling the effects of Ulbricht's failed policies, which pushed the population to meet unrealistic production quotas, deprived them of many non-luxury consumer goods, nationalized industry and organized collective agricultural schemes which failed to yield sufficient produce.

Between the summer of 1952 and the spring of the following year more than 130,000 East Germans applied for permission to emigrate to the West through the Berlin corridor, an exodus which only provoked the DDR to increase production quotas and make life even more intolerable for the remaining inhabitants.

Even Ulbricht's Soviet paymasters thought this was political suicide and strongly advised him to ease up, as the mass defections were becoming a source of embarrassment. There was also a real fear in Moscow that dissent in East Germany could ignite revolt in the surrounding satellite states. In the event, Ulbricht stubbornly refused to back down and instead hardened his line, demanding that production should be increased by 25 per cent. This inevitably led to discontent among the lower-paid workers, who on 16 June 1953 organized an unofficial strike which swiftly evolved into a popular anti-government movement to challenge the authority of the regime.

The Politburo under Premier Khrushchev, Stalin's successor, ordered Russian tanks on to the streets of Berlin and other East German cities where rioting had broken out. Ulbricht authorized the secret police to suppress all protests, violent or otherwise, and the world stood by and watched while the

Soviets demonstrated their authority. More than 200 protestors were killed and 5,000 were arrested, interrogated and jailed.

By the mid-1950s, a third of the prison population in the GDR, some 13,000 individuals, were political prisoners. The West was seen to be impotent, or more accurately paralyzed by the fear that its intervention could trigger a third world war.

Those who had brought down the Iron Curtain were now seen to also possess an iron fist. In 1956, the world would witness a similar demonstration of power in Hungary, to quash a popular uprising, with the loss of 4,000 lives, and again in Czechoslovakia in the late 1960s. It would be more than 20 years before cracks began to appear in the Iron Curtain and the Soviet state finally lost its steely grip on its citizens.

Incredible as it may seem to us now, the name of Auschwitz was unknown to the German public until a team of Frankfurt lawyers defied their superiors to bring the first prosecution of former SS men before a German court in the mid-1960s.

In 1958 Fritz Bauer, an ex-lawyer imprisoned by the Nazis, was appointed Attorney General in the state of Hesse and decided to bring the camp commandant and a number of SS guards to face justice in Germany. But he was up against a conspiracy of silence within sections of the post-war administration and the collective amnesia of the general population.

The crimes committed at Auschwitz were perpetrated in Poland outside the jurisdiction of German courts, so the federal court had to be convinced that the interests of justice would be served by authorizing the regional court of Hesse to indict the accused. The defendants would seek to evade personal responsibility by claiming they were soldiers acting under orders and the testimony of surviving witnesses was assumed to be unreliable after 20 years. Furthermore, German law required irrefutable evidence of murder. Mere cruelty was not considered to be a serious enough offence. Eight thousand SS men had served at the camp from May 1940 to its liberation in January 1945 and identifying those who had committed individual acts of murder was thought to be practically impossible. They had melted into the community, leaving Bauer and his small team of young, idealistic lawyers (Georg Friedrich Vogel, Joachim Kugler and Gerhard Wiese) to track them down.

But the Nazis' obsession with documenting every detail of their operation and recording each transaction provided the necessary proof, and the spurious defence of obeying orders was dismissed after Bauer argued that no one had the right to be obedient, meaning that everyone, even a soldier, has the right to refuse an immoral order. Moreover, several of the accused were shown to have acted on their own initiative.

In all, 22 former SS members appeared in the dock to answer charges before a packed court, including the world's press, although only 17 were ultimately convicted and received nominal sentences. But the trial was not just about the fate of the guilty individuals. It was to put on record what had taken place at Auschwitz and other concentration camps and to give surviving victims a voice. German schoolchildren and students were among the 20,000 attendees who heard harrowing testimony from eyewitnesses, and so over the course of the trial – which ran from 20 December 1963 until 19 August 1965 – the conspiracy of silence was finally broken and the German public forced to confront it past.

## Conclusion

The end of the Second World War saw the emergence of the two global superpowers – the United States and the Soviet Union. The flashpoint was the divided city of Berlin. The former capital of the Third Reich was, in the words of Martin Luther King, Jr, 'the hub around which turns the wheel of history'. An estimated 200 East German citizens were killed attempting to cross the minefield and scale the 12-foot-high wall (3.7m) begun in 1961. The division of Berlin and its subsequent encirclement with the 87-mile-long (140 kilometres) wall became a symbol of Soviet repression and its construction signalled the end of cooperation between the Four Powers (the United States, Britain, France and the Soviet Union).

This hostile stalemate lasted for over 45 years until the fall of the Berlin Wall in November 1989 and the collapse of the Soviet Union two years later, in December 1991. In 1945, Germany's armed forces had been defeated and the symbols of National Socialism removed and consigned to history, but the legacy of Adolf Hitler's Third Reich remains with us to this day in the form of racism, xenophobia and extremism in all its forms. As Hannah Arendt wrote in *Origins of Totalitarianism*:

*... if there is such a thing as a totalitarian personality or mentality [...] extraordinary adaptability and absence of continuity are no doubt its outstanding characteristics. Hence it might be a mistake to assume that the inconstancy and forgetfulness of the masses signify that they are cured of the totalitarian delusion ... The opposite might well be true.*

# ACKNOWLEDGEMENTS

## Documentaries
*Germany After the War* (BBC)
*The World at War* (Thames Television, 1973)

## Resources
BBC.com
bergenbelsen.co.uk
CWM Knowles howitreallywas.typepad.com
Dannyreviews.com
Derspiegel.de
Facinghistory.org
Markfelton.co.uk
Open.edu
The *Spectator*

## Bibliography
Andreas-Friedrich, Ruth *Berlin Underground* (Paragon, 1989)
         —— *Battleground Berlin* (Paragon, 1990)
Baker, Kevin *General Discontent* (American Heritage, 2002)
Beevor, Antony *The Fall of Berlin* (Penguin, 2003)
Charles River Editors *East Germany* (Charles River Editors, 2017)
Churchill, Winston *The Sinews of Peace* (The Churchill Centre, 2015)
Douglas, R.M. *Orderly and Humane: The Expulsion of the Germans after the Second World War* (Yale University Press, 2012)
Evans, Richard *The Third Reich at War* (Penguin, 2009)
Feigel, Lara *The Bitter Taste of Victory* (Bloomsbury, 2016)
Heck, Alfons *Child of Hitler* (Primer, 1985)
Herwig, Malte *Post-War Lies* (Scribe, 2013)
Judt, Tony *Postwar – A History of Europe Since 1945* (Vintage, 2010)
Knowles, Christopher *Winning the Peace* (Bloomsbury, 2017)

Large, David Clay *Berlin* (Basic Books, 2000)

Leonard, Angela *Access to History: Germany Divided and Reunited* (Hodder, 2009)

Macdonagh, Giles *After the Reich* (John Murray, 2008)

Sebestyen, Victor *1946: The Making of the Modern World* (Macmillan, 2014)

Stargardt, Nicholas *Witnesses of War* (Pimlico, 2006)

Taylor, Frederick *Exorcising Hitler* (Bloomsbury, 2012)

Windsor, Philip *A City on Leave* (Chatto and Windus, 1963)

de Zayas, Alfred *A Terrible Revenge* (St Martin's Press, 2006)

# INDEX

## IMAGES

All images: Getty images